demi lovato
&
selena gomez
the complete unofficial story of the BFFs

demi lovato & selena gomez

the complete unofficial story of the BFFs

LUCY RUTHERFORD

ECW Press

Published by ECW Press, 2120 Queen Street East, Suite 200, Toronto, Ontario, Canada M4E 1E2
416.694.3348 / info@ecwpress.com

LIBRARY AND ARCHIVES CANADA CATALOGUING IN PUBLICATION

Rutherford, Lucy
Demi Lovato & Selena Gomez: the complete unofficial story of the BFFs / Lucy Rutherford.

ISBN-13: 978-1-55022-901-1
ISBN-10: 1-55022-901-X

1. Lovato, Demi, 1992– — Juvenile literature. 2. Gomez, Selena, 1992– — Juvenile literature. 3. Actors — United States — Biography — Juvenile literature. I. Title.

PN2287.L68 R88 2009   J791.4302'80922   C2009-901431-9

Cover design: Rachel Ironstone
Text layout and design: Tania Craan
Printing: Transcontinental   1   2   3   4   5

The publication of *Demi Lovato & Selena Gomez* has been generously supported by the OMDC Book Fund, an initiative of the Ontario Media Development Corporation, by the Government of Ontario through the Ontario Book Publishing Tax Credit, and by the Government of Canada through the Book Publishing Industry Development Program (BPIDP).

Canadä

INTRODUCTION

Many parents believe their children have star quality. Audition calls for young talent are met with hundreds, sometimes thousands, of responses. Casting offices are brimming with children whose parents are convinced they've raised the next Miley Cyrus or Raven-Symoné. So, what makes one child stand out from all the other wannabe stars?

For years, kids ages seven to thirteen had few stars they could call their own. Known as the "tween" demographic, their stories and concerns were rarely the focus of Hollywood scripts or lyrics. Disney saw an opening. "We found there was this huge demo that was too old for Nickelodeon and too young for MTV," says Anne Sweeney, president of Disney-ABC Television Group. "We realized this was an opportunity for Disney to establish itself in the lives of these kids."

Disney Channel is a cable network created in 1983. During its early years, the network carried some original programming, including the sitcom *Kids Incorporated*, but also relied heavily on reruns and popular Disney movies to fill airtime. In 1989, Disney revived *The Mickey Mouse Club*, the popular variety show performed by kids for kids, which aired in the 1950s and briefly reappeared in the 1970s. *The All-New Mickey Mouse Club* launched the careers of an impressive number of stars, including Christina Aguilera, JC Chasez, Ryan Gosling, Britney Spears, and Justin Timberlake. But it wasn't until the 2000s, when Anne Sweeney came on board, that Disney Channel found its footing. The new decade debuted hit after hit, starting with *The Proud Family*, and building audiences with *Even Stevens* and *Lizzie McGuire*. In 2005, *That's So Raven* became the network's highest-rated series of all time.

Disney Channel has also scored big with original movies, most notably 2006's smash hit *High School Musical* — the most successful Disney Channel movie to date, with more than 7 million viewers. The following year, an astonishing 17.2 million viewers took in its sequel, making *High School Musical 2* both the highest-rated cable and the highest-rated made-for-TV movie ever. *High School Musical 3: Senior Year*, which was released in movie theaters, broke the record for the largest opening weekend for a musical film. Legions of devoted fans have turned *HSM* into a huge franchise, gobbling up more than 8 million CDs, 8 million DVDs, and 9 million tie-in novels, as well as video games and tickets to the stage musical, ice show, and sold-out concert tour.

On March 24, 2006, 5.4 million viewers tuned in to watch the debut of Disney's *Hannah Montana* — a family comedy series starring 14-year-old Miley Cyrus and her country music star dad, Billy Ray Cyrus — the highest ratings ever for a kids' series premiere. The show spawned CDs, DVDs, a concert tour that sold out instantly, a 3D concert documentary, and a book series, among countless product tie-ins. A feature film was released in April 2009 and immediately became a huge hit. When Miley brought the Jonas Brothers along on tour in fall 2007, the brothers went from having a modest but fiercely devoted audience to becoming a household name.

Hannah Montana set off a tidal wave of winning shows in 2008, including *Phineas and Ferb, The Suite Life on Deck* (a spin-off to the wildly successful series *The Suite Life of Zack & Cody*), and *Wizards of Waverly Place*. Original movies held their own, with major hits such as *The Cheetah Girls: One World, Minutemen,* and *Camp Rock*.

Each success has relied heavily on the charisma of Disney's stars. "The Disney Channel is probably the greatest teen-star incubator since the NBA stopped drafting high schoolers," wrote Karl Taro Greenfeld in *Conde Naste Portfolio Magazine*.

Unquestionably, a large part of their fans' loyalty comes from a burning aspiration to be like these young celebs. From their devotion to God to their favorite brand of sneakers, the enchanted lives of Disney stars are closely followed in dozens of glossy magazines and fansites. Yet, audiences also have to believe that "'this is someone who could be my friend. This is the girl who could be next to me in math class, and we could do our homework together,'" according to *Teen Magazine*'s entertainment editor Kelly Bryant. "They have this extraordinary life in our readers' eyes because they're on TV, and they're in movies, and they're recording albums, but at the same time, it seems like someone that they could hang out with."

It's a tall order for any teenager to be talented, stylish, attractive, and morally upright, while still relatable to ordinary folks. Millions of kids might want the job, but few are truly qualified. So, where exactly do you find someone like that?

fated to be friends

"I always knew that one day, somehow,
I'd be here where I am today . . .
Or, at least, I was dreaming it."
— Demi

Selena with her mom, Mandy, her stepdad, Brian Teefey, and one of her best friends, Randy Hill, a skateboarder Selena has known since she was five. "I can always go to him when I need someone to talk to," she says. "I've known him my whole life. I know everything about him, and he's sweet."

Few celebrities have climbed the rungs of the entertainment industry as seemingly quickly as Demi Lovato and Selena Gomez. Their rise to stardom has appeared so brisk that

some might describe them as overnight successes — twin Cinderella stories. But both girls have been in the business since they were very young. Both are multi-talented — accomplished as actors, singers, musicians, and dancers — and showed a determination to "make it" from an early age. Just as importantly, Demi and Selena possess qualities that have made millions of fans want to be their friends. For all their talent and ambition, for all the bright lights and glamour that now surround them, they still appear to be ordinary girls who have remained true to their roots — and to each other.

Little girl of Grand Prairie

Selena Marie Gomez was born in New York on July 22, 1992, but was raised in Grand Prairie, Texas, about 15 miles from Dallas. Her mother, Mandy, was just 16 when she had Selena. She separated from Selena's father, Ricardo Gomez, five years later, marrying Selena's stepfather, Brian Teefey, in 2006.

Selena was immersed in show business as a little girl. "My mom did a lot of theater when I was younger so I grew up around it, and I just always loved it," Selena says. "I loved running lines with her."

While her mother may have instilled a passion for acting in Selena, it was her father who set her destiny as a singer. Mexican-born Ricardo named his daughter after the late Mexican-American singer Selena Quintanilla-Pérez. The Latina songstress was often called the "Queen of Tejano Music," but to her fans she was simply Selena. Like Selena Gomez, Selena grew up in the public eye: she was just 12 when her first album came out. She quickly rose to superstardom within the Hispanic music industry, winning Female Vocalist of the Year at the 1987 Tejano Music Awards. In 1995, she was on the cusp of launching an English-language career when she was shot and killed by the president of her fan club. She was 23 years old. Two weeks later, then-Governor George W. Bush declared April 12 to be "Selena Day" in Demi and Selena's home state of Texas.

Of her namesake, Selena Gomez has said, "I kind of think that . . . I'm the reincarnation of her."

Selena Quintanilla-Pérez is Selena's namesake, pictured here five months before her death. The name Selena is Greek; Selena was the Greek goddess of the moon.

Kindergarten crooner

Demetria Devonne Lovato was born on August 20, 1992, to Patrick and Dianna Lovato, and raised in Colleyville, Texas, near Dallas. As her name suggests, Demi is of Hispanic and Italian descent (with a bit of Irish too).

Demi's mother, a former country music singer and Dallas Cowboys cheerleader, is such a hometown girl that she even named the Lovatos' first child, Demi's older sister, after her birthplace. Dallas is four years older than her famous sibling. The sisters have always been close, perhaps in part because their parents' marriage ended when they were so young — Demi was just a toddler. Shortly afterward, Patrick moved to New Mexico to be closer to his father, Frank Lovato. In 1995, Dianna married Eddie De La Garza, taking his last name. Their daughter, Madison, was born in 2001.

The middle sister of the Lovato–De La Garza family showed an appetite for applause from an early age. "[Demi] was a ham," her mother, Dianna, recalls. "She loved to make people laugh and always wanted to be the center of attention."

Demi's mother and stepfather encouraged her love of the spotlight. She competed in pageants for little girls, winning the Texas Cinderella State Mini Miss pageant in 2000. Dianna says, "It was more about talent and interviews than rhinestones and makeup." No doubt these early experiences primed Demi for a life in front of crowds and cameras.

When Demi was just five years old, she had a revelatory moment at a kindergarten talent show. She was performing "My Heart Will Go On," Celine Dion's soaring ballad from the movie *Titanic*, when her microphone stopped working. A boy sitting in the front row of the audience started making faces at her, and she momentarily forgot the words to the song. Tears flooded Demi's eyes. It was a bad dream come true — but she carried on. "I just kept it up," she remembers. "And at that moment, when I stuck through it and stopped crying on stage, I guess that's when I realized, 'Wow, I don't hate this enough to run off.'"

At an age when most children are still

As a child, Demi featured in several child beauty pageants, which gave her the experience of being on stage at a very young age.

learning to tie their shoes, Demi had found her career path. "It actually clicked in my head," she says. "I decided I wanted to be a singer."

Four-year-old Demi (right) with her older sister Dallas, who is also a singer and actor.

A Survivor

Demi's grandfather, Frank Lovato, is an American national hero. He is one of the survivors of the brutal Bataan Death March that happened in 1942, where the Japanese forcibly marched 76,000 American and Filipino prisoners of war for 90 miles. It is estimated that anywhere from a quarter to a third of the prisoners died on the march. Demi's uncle, Francisco Lovato, has published an account of Frank Lovato's heroic experience in a book called *Survivor*. Demi's grandfather has watched her career with much admiration over the years, and he is very proud of what his granddaughter has achieved.

Demi with her stepdad, Eddie De La Garza (who is also her manager), and her mother, Dianna, a former Dallas Cowboys cheerleader.

The format of the show has remained fairly consistent over the years. A cast of precocious children hang out with the big, purple dinosaur, playing games, solving common problems, and singing songs about friendship, manners, and other life lessons. In 1998, *Barney* producers were looking for new talent to add to their stable of young actors. Demi had tried out at a local casting call the year before. She was turned down because at age five, "I didn't know how to read yet." Now she was back for a second chance, and her future best friend was standing in line with her, even though she didn't know it yet.

"It was scorching hot, July," Selena told *Entertainment Weekly*. "We were in line with 1,400 kids and we happened to be standing right next to each other. She had a little bow in her hair, and she turned around and she looked at me and said, 'Do you want to color?' She laid her blue jean jacket down and we started to color."

The girls both received callbacks — an opportunity to re-audition. With each callback, the number of actors in contention is whittled down. During one callback, the girls ran into each other again, and as Selena tells it, their friendship was reignited with just a look. Selena remembers, "I saw [Demi] from the other side of the room and it was kind of a movie moment. We still joke about it."

Both girls landed roles, and were series regulars for the next two seasons, Selena playing Gianna and Demi playing Angela.

Learning the ropes

They say "everything is bigger in Texas," and that is certainly true of the larger-than-life television phenomenon that was born in the southwestern state. Barney, the television T-Rex that has entertained millions of preschoolers, was created in Dallas in 1987. The show began as a collection of videos, and became a regular series on PBS called *Barney & Friends* in 1992. It is now broadcast around the world.

Barney has been played by a few actors over the years. When Demi and Selena were on *Barney & Friends*, David Joyner donned the purple suit while Bob West provided the dinosaur's voice on the show and albums.

In video clips, Selena is the easier of the two to pick out. She has the same distinctive heart-shaped face and large brown eyes, and is nearly as clear spoken and comfortable on camera then as she is today. Demi is a little quieter and seems less sure of herself, although she sings with confidence. Beneath her glasses, her cherubic face has yet to lose its baby fat, and she has a small gap between her teeth, which she had filled in as a teenager. (Selena has said she tried to talk Demi out of fixing her teeth; she liked them the way they were.)

Most teenagers cringe when old childhood pictures are put on public display, never mind YouTube videos of them dancing with a purple dinosaur. But Selena has nothing but fondness for her *Barney* days. "It's such a wonderful memory to me," she says. "A lot of people would be embarrassed to say they were on *Barney* but I embrace the fact and I had such a wonderful time doing that show."

Barney also provides a valuable training ground for the gifted children who join the cast, an experience both girls would draw on in the years to come. "I learned everything from *Barney*," Selena says. "Stage directions, camera angles . . . I even learned good manners. Saying 'please' and 'thank you' became a habit."

chapter 2
a whole new world

"I'm a Texas girl at heart."
— Selena

Selena

"My mom is my best friend," Selena says. "She's always with me everywhere I go. Sometimes on set, I just need to see her face. I'm like, 'Mom, I need to see you.' I just have to have my mom."

Selena loves to eat lemons — sliced with a bit of salt. Her **Wizards** mother, Maria Canals-Barrera, thinks it's hilarious, but it drives Selena's real mom crazy. "My mom is getting on me for that because it's bad for my teeth," she says. "But I'm like, 'I brush every day, every night,' and she's like, 'It doesn't matter. It's going to get your enamel.' She's getting all mad at me."

After two seasons on *Barney & Friends*, Selena had outgrown the show; the time had come to replace her with a younger actress. The producers "felt like I was getting a little too old, so I got the boot," she says.

Selena was quickly outgrowing her home state, as well. There were more opportunities outside of Texas — in New York or Los Angeles — but Selena's family wasn't going to uproot itself unless the right opportunity came along.

Selena kept working, acting in commercials for companies such as Wal-Mart, Hasbro, and TGI Friday's. The year 2003 brought a small supporting role in Walt Disney Pictures' feature film *Spy Kids 3D: Game Over*. Dressed in a salmon-colored coat, brown satin hat, and Mary Jane shoes, Selena played the haughty client of Juni Cortez, a young private eye played by Daryl Sabara. They would meet again when Daryl guest-starred on Selena's career-making show, but the setting for that reunion was still on the distant horizon.

Friendly competition

Meanwhile, Selena and Demi were still tight. They often studied together after they both began homeschooling, and went to auditions together, as well. In fact, Demi's mother, who is now close friends with Selena's mom, took the girls to the audition that changed Selena's life.

In 2004, the girls traveled to Austin to attend a massive talent search organized by the Disney Channel. Selena was plucked from among the thousands of kids who tried out, and network casting directors immediately began looking for the right project for her.

Demi returned home empty-handed. "Selena and I aren't competitive," she says. "We've talked about it and we've known since we were young that we have the same image. We're both Hispanic and have dark hair, it's just one of those things. . . . My

Selena at the premiere of *Shrek the Third*.

Selena hams it up with Dylan and Cole Sprouse at her 16th birthday party.

original show played by Lalaine Vergara-Paras. Selena landed the plum part of the title character, Stephanie "Stevie" Sanchez, Miranda's sister.

Unfortunately, in the television business, only a handful of pilots go on to become shows. The stars of the television series *Friends* — one of Selena's all-time favorites — have all said they worked on many pilots before landing the roles that would turn them into household names and multi-millionaires. *What's Stevie Thinking?* was not one of the lucky ones. Selena's big break was yet to come.

Brain Zapped

In 2005, Selena made a brief appearance on the television series *Walker, Texas Ranger* alongside Mitchel Musso. In an episode titled "Trial by Fire," they portrayed the playmates of a missing boy at the heart of the show's storyline. Mitchel would soon become known for his goofy portrayal of Oliver Oken on the Disney Channel's *Hannah Montana*.

The following year, Selena played Emily Grace Garcia in the pilot episode of *Brain Zapped*, produced by EGG Entertainment. Written, directed, and produced by Eliud George Garcia, *Brain Zapped* is about the otherworldly adventures of a young bibliophile who is transported from the local library to fantastical faraway places and time periods. She is accompanied by her best friend, Kingston, played by Lewis Parry.

mom would say if one of us gets something it's better than none of us getting something. So whoever gets it, we're happy for each other."

With the same "that's life" attitude, Demi's mother later told the *Wall Street Journal*, "Selena is an adorable-looking Hispanic girl, and looks more Hispanic than Demi, and that's what they were looking for at the time."

Selena was cast in *What's Stevie Thinking?*, a spin-off of the hugely popular television show *Lizzie McGuire*, which starred Hilary Duff. The series in development focused on the family of Miranda Sanchez, a supporting character from the

18

Much of *Brain Zapped* was filmed in front of a green screen that was later filled in with special effects images; Selena and Lewis had to imagine flying through space and encountering dinosaurs. It was a good learning experience for Selena, which she would use in the years to come. But besides being shown at children's festivals as if it were a movie, it didn't go anywhere.

Hanging out at the Mouse House

During the two years following her audition in Austin, Disney kept Selena close by. In 2006, she made a guest appearance on the Emmy Award–nominated *The Suite Life of Zack & Cody*, which was produced from 2005 to 2008 (Zack and Cody live on in the high-seas spin-off, *The Suite Life on Deck*). Starring Dylan and Cole Sprouse, the series revolved around the shenanigans of twin brothers living at the Tipton Hotel. A noticeably taller and leaner Selena played Gwen, Cody's fleeting love interest. She also appeared on another spin-off of *The Suite Life of Zack & Cody* revolving around Arwin, the handy man at the Tipton Hotel. That pilot, too, was destined for the cutting room floor. But Selena's luck was about to improve.

Few people need to be introduced to the marvel that is *Hannah Montana*. The runaway success, which premiered on the Disney Channel in March 2006, stars Miley Cyrus as Miley Stewart, a supposedly average teen who leads a double life as the pop star Hannah Montana. Only Miley's family — including her father, played by real-life dad Billy Ray Cyrus — and her two best friends know Hannah Montana's true identity.

When Selena arrived on the set, *Hannah Montana* was already a hit. Selena played pop star Mikayla, Hannah's arch nemesis, in three episodes. Mikayla has had only one top ten hit, "If Cupid Had a Heart," and is fiercely jealous of Hannah's many smashes. Hannah calls her "Mik-cockroach" and "a two-faced, tone-deaf toad." Mikayla calls Hannah "Has Been," which prompts the retort: "Never Was!"

Stylish and polished but razor-tongued and completely self-absorbed, Mikayla is a far cry from the wholesome image Selena had always projected. Selena was wickedly good at being wicked, if not always totally comfortable with the sharp barbs she delivered. "Me and Miley would do a scene where we're mad and saying mean things, and when they'd cut, we would run up to

On *Hannah Montana*, Selena played Hannah's rival, Mikayla.

each other and say, 'I'm so sorry,'" Selena recalls. "People would laugh and they're like, 'You're just acting,' and we're like, 'I know, but I feel so bad.'"

In one memorable episode, titled "That's What Friends Are For?," Mikayla takes up with Miley's former boyfriend, famous teen actor Jake Ryan (played by Cody Linley). What begins as an onscreen love affair in a movie threatens to develop into the real deal, much to Miley's horror. Miley is too embarrassed to admit to Jake that she's jealous, so she concocts a hair-brained scheme to keep her rival and her ex apart. She's busted, of course, but in spite of Miley's attempted sabotage, Mikayla wants to become friends with her. In fact, she enlists Miley in the war against Hannah, kicking off a whole new complication.

Mikayla was enormously popular with *Hannah Montana* fans; there was no question Disney had a hot property on its hands, and was determined to find the right spot for her. The wait was almost over: the hit maker was about to work its magic once again.

Homesick

The move from Grand Prairie to Los Angeles was bittersweet for Selena. "It was hard," she recalls. "It was almost a test of how badly I really wanted to pursue acting. Which I did, there was no question in my mind that I wanted to come out here and do this. But it was really tough to leave my friends behind."

"Without Disney, we wouldn't be out here at all," Selena's mother, Mandy, told a reporter shortly after she moved with Selena to Los Angeles. (Stepdad Brian kept the home fires burning in Texas until the family was ready to make a permanent move.) "We're a paycheck-to-paycheck family, and they kept paying for everything. I feel guilty sometimes."

She needn't have worried; Disney had made this investment many times before. Grooming a young talent for stardom is a long process. The network needs to make

Regular pilgrimages to Selena's home state of Texas ease the culture shock this Grand Prairie girl sometimes experiences in Los Angeles. "I miss walking," she says, of living in the Pacific city. "I used to walk barefoot around my neighborhood without worrying about anything. It's nice and peaceful. We could walk in the middle of the street, and there would be no cars coming at all. In L.A., you can't do that."

sure that the up-and-comers are prepared for the thrilling but highly demanding life ahead and that their families are behind them. Disney makes fewer pilots than other networks — a higher percentage of them go on to become shows — and work hard to match each actor or singer with the right project at the right time.

Still, in spite of Disney's faith in her future, it was a challenging time for Selena and her family, caught between their old life back in Texas but not quite ready to set up house in California. "Leaving my dad and moving away from the rest of my family was scary," she says. "It was like, I had good *and* freaked out feelings at the same time. It was probably the most scared I've ever been in my whole life. . . . But I knew I had to come to California and that it would be okay because I was doing what I always wanted to do. And the people I love, like my dad and friends, would come out and visit me — or I could go back to visit them!"

demi's star rises

"I'm definitely very ambitious . . .
I've always known I was supposed
to do this, ever since I was really,
really young. I saw what I wanted in
my dreams, and then I worked hard."
– Demi

The cast of *As the Bell Rings*, which is filmed near Austin, Texas. From left to right: Carlson Young, Seth Ginsberg, Demi, Tony Oller, Collin Cole, and Gabriella Rodriguez. Demi and Tony Oller recorded the original song "Shadow" for the show.

Demi kept busy after her stint on *Barney*. She guest-starred on shows such as *Prison Break* and *Just Jordan*. She appeared as herself on a reality series called *Split Ends* in which two hairstylists switch salons, introducing their signature techniques to their new clientele (a similar concept to shows like *Wife Swap*). One of the stylists gave Demi's hair a real "pageant treatment."

In 2006, Demi once again auditioned for the Disney Channel at a talent search in Dallas. This time, she had the qualities the casting directors were looking for, and landed the part of Charlotte Adams on Disney Channel's brand new show *As the Bell Rings*. Demi was the female lead for its first season. At the time it may have seemed like the first of many steps toward fulfilling

her dreams. Little did Demi know, the short-format show would help vault her to the big time.

Demi goes Disney

If the show's title has a familiar "ring" to it, that's because it deliberately echoes the long-running soap opera *As the World Turns*. As any student knows, most of the melodrama (and comedy) in a school day happens in the moments between classes. Each of *As the Bell Rings*' five-minute episodes, which air between Disney's longer-format shows, takes place in front of

Demi loves extra-gooey homemade Rice Krispie treats and oranges.

the hallway window, and starts and ends with the class bell ringing.

"Even though the show was only five minutes, it was the Disney Channel!" Demi says. "I thought it was the coolest thing." It was also the scariest. "When I got the part, I actually cried," she recalls. "I thought, I'm not going to be able to do this — I'm not funny! I'm never going to be able to work for the Disney Channel, because they're based on comedy."

Over the course of season one, viewers watched a slow-blooming romance develop between Charlotte and Danny, played by Tony Oller. Danny's goofball sidekicks Toejam (Seth Ginsberg) and Skipper (Collin Cole) provide much of the comic relief on the show, although Tiffany Blake (Carlson Young), a pretty and popular but hopelessly clueless blond, gets her share of laughs. Brooke Nichols (Gabriella Rodriguez) rounds out the ensemble as the brains of the bunch.

Different versions of As the Bell Rings have been produced all over the world. The first was on Disney's Italian channel and called Quelli dell'intervallo. In season two, Charlotte moved away and Lindsey Black took over as the lead female, playing Lexi, sparking a new romance with Danny.

"You saved me"

In November 2008, Demi wrote on her MySpace blog: "I've been talking to a few fans lately and i've been fortunate enough to maintain a friendship with them over myspace or emails and even though our lives are completely different, we still have one thing in common; having trouble dealing with the cruelty of others. or some people call it bullying. i've dealt with it before until i made the decision to homeschool but sometimes it seems as if it doesn't just end in high-school. sometimes i get online and read blogs (which i probably shouldn't if i can't handle it) and read the horrible things that people say in comments... and it can really take a toll on you. verbal abuse can be just as harmful as physical abuse. the fans that i have stayed in touch tell me all the time that they're either being harassed online or being beaten at school and it hurts me to hear that. i took the easy road out and decided to homeschool but unfortunately not everyone has that option. so as a message to everyone.. please keep in mind when you're about to threaten someone, make fun of them or leave blog comments about them.... that what you say or do to others can truly affect someone. and as cheesy and lame as it may sound.. never forget the golden rule. and by the way. i wanted to say how thankful i am for you all. I'm so honored to be in the position that I'm in. you all have saved me."

Even stars can be bullied

Demi's own school life didn't run as smoothly as Charlotte's. Being beautiful, talented, and on TV may have made Demi famous, but it didn't make her popular. In fact, the more famous Demi became, the harder it got to hang out with regular kids. "I asked to leave public school," she admits. "I was kind of bullied. I had a hate wall in the bathroom, and everyone signed a petition that said 'We all hate Demi Lovato.'"

Today, Demi believes the other kids might have been jealous of her success. "I never really understood why [I was being bullied] until looking back," she says. "I had a different lifestyle than everyone else."

Demi says she has a better perspective on things now, although she still hates the teenage-girl cat fights captured in movies like *Mean Girls*. "I've been through a lot, probably more than most girls, but I think that it's just trying to look at the positive and not falling into the trap of losing yourself to peer pressure," she says.

Homeschooling was, she admits, "lonely at first, but also I probably couldn't go back to high school just because I see through a lot."

Selena was invaluable during the tough times. "Keep a good friend close," Demi says of her best friend. "I left school because of mean girls. Selena was my one and only friend. She totally stood up for me. It's the same with me. If you mess with my friends, I don't really know if I'm going to be that nice to you."

Selena has had her share of troubles, too. A group of girls spread rumors about her that badly damaged her reputation. She turned the other cheek. "You can't get involved, fire back or do anything," the starlet says. "If people say 'I heard you did this,' just say, 'I'm sorry, that's not true!'" She adds, "At the end of the day, I really ended up finding out who my true friends were."

Demi regularly speaks out about bullying, including a high-profile interview about the experience on *The Ellen DeGeneres Show*. "I want to help with bullying," she told the talk show host, "because there are girls who can't just up and homeschool and focus on their career."

chapter 4
selena finds magic

"I love playing [Alex]. She is very confident in what she believes in and stands up for it even though it may not be right. I think we are similar in that way. Other than that, I don't think I could have the sassy quality. My parents would never like that." – Selena

In "Harper Knows," the Russos go on special assignment at PopCon, the popular comic book and movie convention, watching for rogue wizards who may be using their magic. From left to right: Selena, Jennifer Stone, David Henrie, Jake T. Austin, Maria Canals-Barrera, and David DeLuise.

Selena finally found the right home on Disney — in the comfortable living room of the Russo family. The fictional Russos live in the Waverly neighborhood of New York City. Like many families these days, they represent a blend of cultures: Mrs. Russo is Hispanic and Mr. Russo is . . . a wizard. Behind closed doors, their children — Alex, Justin, and Max — are preparing for an ultimate contest of their magic pow-

ers. Only one of the three will be able to keep their wizardry skills when they grow up, and they aren't shy about getting in each other's way. When their father isn't teaching Wizard Class, he's running the family restaurant — Waverly Sub Station — while he and his wife try to keep up with the antics of three young wizards-in-training.

The idea for *Wizards of Waverly Place* originated with Todd J. Greenwald, a writer for *Hannah Montana*. Disney involved Selena in the show's development early on, and she had a lot of input into her character, Alex Russo. "When we began working on it, I wanted to be the tomboy character and maybe have a girly best friend — flip it around from the usual thing," she says. "I used the inspiration of some of my favorite shows, like *Friends*, took some comedy from there, and they liked it."

In the series premiere, which aired on October 12, 2007, Alex uses a duplicating spell to make a copy of herself so she can skip wizard training to shop at a sale. Panic (and laughter) ensues when her mother appears at the store. "There are always times when you wish you could be invisible when something embarrassing happens," Selena said, shortly before the Sunday-night sitcom debuted. "Or you wish you could rewind time because you just tripped in front of everybody. That's why I think kids

Jake T. Austin with his little sister, Ava.

"My favorite scenes are ones where all of the family is together," Selena says. "Whether it's a funny or dramatic scene, whether we're trying to solve a problem or doing magic or turning my brother invisible, it comes off best when we're with the whole family in the loft. I think when we're all together the show is at its strongest point. And I love being with the entire cast in a scene."

will like the show. We bring to life everything that they imagine and dream about."

Jake T. Austin

"The Russo family is sort of like my family in real life," says Jake T. Austin, who plays the youngest member of the wizard crew, Max. Born in 1994 in New York, Jake T.'s birth name is Jake Toranzo-Szymanski, reflecting his mother's Argentinean and Puerto Rican roots, and his father's Polish and Irish heritage. "The mother [on *Wizards*] is Spanish like my mom, and the father is not Spanish — like my dad," he says. "I can relate to that."

Max is a bit of a rascal (although his quick thinking has gotten the Russo siblings out of some tight jams), his impulsive personality contrasting with the industrious and ambitious young actor who plays him. During *Wizards'* first season Jake T. was also heard as the voice of Diego on Nickelodeon's preschool show *Go, Diego, Go!*, which he joined at age nine. He has also done voice work for two animated feature films, *Everyone's Hero* and *The Ant Bully*, and starred in the Disney Channel original movie *Johnny Kapahala: Back on Board*. In January 2009, Jake T. starred in *Hotel for Dogs*, and has signed on for *The Perfect Game*, which begins production in 2009. The new film was inspired by the first non-U.S. team to win the Little League World Series. No slouch in the music department either, Jake T. sings on the album *Diego, Dora & Friends Animal Jamboree*.

David Henrie

"I had a terrible first audition," admits David Henrie, who plays the oldest Russo sibling, Justin. "It was horrible. I didn't know my stuff. I was missing all my beats and I wasn't funny. I walked out of there thinking I will never work for Disney again, but somehow I got a callback for it and I nailed it."

Born in 1989 in Los Angeles, David spent part of his childhood in Arizona. He credits his love for the spotlight to competing for attention within his extended family, which includes his younger brother Lorenzo and many cousins. "Growing up in such a large, LOUD Italian family it was easy to get overlooked," he has written. "So I made sure I kept everyone entertained for as long as possible."

Older and wiser than his siblings — although not totally immune to mischief — Justin Russo has many qualities David admires. "I love Justin because the theme in life right now is 'Do what's bad,' like that's cool," David notes on his personal website. "But Justin makes it cool to be a good guy. When someone marches to the beat of their own drum and is totally confident in their own ways and doesn't care what anyone else thinks, that is cool! Justin portrays the characteristics that can help kids who choose to do what is 'right,' lead more confident lives."

That's So Raven! fans will recognize David from his recurring role as Larry on the Disney Channel comedy series. He has

Q: On which CBS sitcom does David Henrie currently moonlight?
Hint: He plays one of the teenagers who are bored to tears by their father's never-ending recollection of their parents' romance.
A: *How I Met Your Mother*

David Henrie with Maria Canals-Barrera. "Minus those people who have made poor decisions, Disney really grooms you to be prepared for network TV or movies," David Henrie says. "You already have experience under your belt in how to handle yourself in public, you're experienced on set, in crunch time you're already more experienced than other people."

also guest-starred on hit shows such as *Cold Case*, *House*, and *Without a Trace*, and had lead roles on the Fox series *Method and Red* and *The Pitts*. In February 2009, David appeared in the Disney original movie *Dadnapped*, in which an unlikely band of teens helps the daughter of a bestselling author rescue her kidnapped father. The movie costars Emily Osment, Moises Arias, and Denzel Dominique Whitaker.

Maria Canals-Barrera

Quick-witted but long-suffering Theresa Russo, the only family member who does not have magical powers, is played by Maria Canals-Barrera. Maria also voices the characters Sunset Boulevardez on the animated series *Proud Family* and Hawkgirl on *The Justice League*, and played Demi's onscreen mom in *Camp Rock* (talk about friends sharing *everything*).

Maria was born in Miami in 1966. She has a background in theater and appeared in feature films such as *America's Sweethearts* and *The Master of Disguise*. Among her many televisions credits are a recurring part on the PBS television series *American Family* and a starring role on *The Tony Danza Show*. She won an Alma Award in 2002 for her role in *Brothers Garcia*. Her guest appearances include stints on *Curb Your Enthusiasm*, *George Lopez*, and *Almost Perfect*.

Maria says the *Wizards* cast "clicked" from the get-go. "In fact, that was one of the reasons that we were cast together, because

33

the chemistry was instant," Maria recalls. "Actually, I remember I went in with Selena, who plays my daughter, and we went in together for one of the last callbacks, and I had already played her mother on another show that didn't go, another pilot. And the chemistry was there."

Maria has much affection for her television husband, with whom she gets along famously. "David DeLuise is just a big old cuddly teddy bear," she says. "I just adore that guy. I really do. When you play somebody's spouse, sometimes you have to really work it, feeling that love. But I don't; I just loved him instantly. He's just adorable and very funny." She adds, "And the kids are terrific. They've got good heads on their shoulders, they're comedically very talented, and it's really in the parenting. They all have great parents, and it shows."

David DeLuise

It may be impossible to imagine anyone else in the role of Jerry Russo, but Selena's television dad, David DeLuise, debated whether he would join the cast. Was he the right actor for the part? While discussing the role with his brother Peter, who is also an actor, David had a revelation. "I was like, 'Oh my god, I love it! I would get to be a kooky dad teaching his kids about magic. It's perfect,'" David says. "I'm really happy to be a part of it. I have a lot of fun. My days are filled with joy now. It's weird how things happen."

David was born into a showbiz family in 1971. His father, Dom, was a well-loved actor, comedian, and director, and his brothers, Peter and Michael, and mother, Carol Arthur, all have impressive acting credits. Before *Wizards*, David was perhaps best known for his roles on the sitcom *3rd Rock from the Sun* and the sci-fi series *Stargate SG-1*. He has also guest-starred on many top shows, from *ER* to *Monk* to *Gilmore Girls* and all three *CSI* series, had a recurring role on a comedy series starring Christina Applegate called *Jesse*, and appeared in several feature films, including the comedies *Robin Hood: Men in Tights* and *Hairshirt*.

David has a special fondness for his television daughter, who continually impresses him. He says, "When I first started working with [Selena], she was obviously two years younger and she had impeccable timing for comedy and I was like, 'Honey, where did you get that, where did it come from?' She's like, 'Well, I've watched every episode of *Friends*.' And I went, 'Okay, well, they have good timing on that show so obviously that's rubbed off on you.'"

What magical power would David like to have in real life? "I think I would have to go with flying," he says. "Just because I live in L.A. and there's so much traffic. I wouldn't mind flying, and picking up my kids and flying home."

After two seasons together, the real-life father of two has nothing but praise for his entire television brood. "Selena, Dave Henrie, and Jake T. are as professional as you can get as a kid actor," David says. "I mean, there's awareness in them that . . . we [can] have a great time but there is work to be done. And you know, sometimes it can get pretty boring standing still when the cameras are getting set up and it just makes everybody's day go that much easier if people are — especially the kids — focused."

Jennifer Stone

Believe it or not, Jennifer Stone is also from Texas. She began her career in theater at age six, moving from Arlington to Los Angeles to look for work in television and film at age nine. "My mom took my brother to find something to do one summer besides play video games," she remembers. "He went for the paper and saw an ad for theater auditions. He went and auditioned and got the lead role and I sort of got dragged to a rehearsal and so I started doing theater. It sort of progressed from there."

"We definitely have our likes and differences," says Jennifer of her character, Harper. "I think I am like her in the fact that I get really excited about silly things . . . I am different in the fact that I am a bit more mellow than she is."

got the call when I was back in my hometown in Texas to fly out the next day," she says. "It was very sudden. . . . Three days later they called and offered me the part."

Harper is an aspiring designer, and donning her wacky wardrobe makes it easy for Jennifer to get into character. "I have a ton of costumes. I open the script every week, and I'm like, 'Okay, what are they going to put me in now?' I've had cupcakes on my head, I've had birds on my hats, I've had all sorts of lip glosses hanging from my skirts; it's been nutso what my character wears."

Jennifer had a small role in the Disney original movie *Dadnapped*, with *Wizards* costar David Henrie (and former costar Haley Joel Osment's sister, Emily). But it is perhaps Selena with whom Jennifer has become closest. "We spend a lot of time together and she is just one of the most amazing human beings I have ever met," Jennifer says. "We laugh because we have gotten to a point where we can be really honest with each other and say what is on our minds and know we won't get reprimanded by the other. I can definitely say she is one of my best friends."

Born in 1993, Jennifer broke into movies when she was cast in New Line Cinema's *Secondhand Lions* alongside Haley Joel Osment. Guest appearances on *House*, *Without a Trace*, and *Line of Fire* kept her busy until she landed the role of Alex Russo's kooky friend Harper at a talent search. "I had done previous work with Disney and

Brothers and besties

Selena and her television brothers are *tight*. "They basically *are* my brothers; they're my real family," Selena says of David Henrie and Jake T. "They're always there for me, and it's torture when I can't see them every day. We do fight like brothers and sisters sometimes, but mostly we play around and

Selena says that David Henrie and Jake T. Austin are like real brothers to her. The three were presenters at the 2008 ALMA Awards.

joke around. I don't have any real-life siblings so this way I can have brothers."

Selena claims would-be suitors should be prepared to go through David and Jake T. if they want to go out with her. "They're both so protective of me. Even when I like a boy or something, they have to make sure he's okay, or the boy has to be 'approved' by them," she says.

The boys might be protective of Selena, but that doesn't mean they don't occasionally turn on each other — all in good fun, of course. "I found [Jake T.'s] phone on set one day, because for some reason he liked to

A look behind the scenes at *Wizards of Waverly Place*. Selena recorded *Wizards'* techno-pop theme song, "Everything Is Not What It Seems," which was written by John Adair and Steve Hampton.

leave it around, and I texted everyone in his phone something I found very funny," David says. "To get me back, he poured parmesan cheese in my car and it melted! It stunk my car up so bad! I had a date that night, making it even worse! So I didn't know what to do to get him back. We were filming a scene one day, in front of a live audience, where his character was holding a cupcake in his hand. I seized the opportu-

nity and shoved it all over his face! It was funnnnn."

Life on the set
One of the challenges for the young acting troupe on *Wizards* is juggling their school-work with the demands of their day jobs. (Actors ages nine to fifteen are legally per-mitted to work only five hours per day on school days.) They study in a shared office

Latina pride

Although neither Selena nor Demi had a *quinceañera* of her own, they take pride in their Hispanic roots. "I love my culture and everything about it," Selena says. "Without it I would not be who I am today."

Selena made history as the first Latina to star in her own Disney Channel series. "Moms come up to me after a show or taping and they say, 'It's so wonderful to see a Latina that my kids can look up to,'" she says. "That makes me feel so proud of where I come from because I do feel like it's a huge step for the Disney Channel to have their first Latin show. It's incredible and I am happy to be a part of that family."

Selena and Maria Canals-Barrera were both nominated for 2008 ALMA Awards, which celebrates Latinos in television, in the Outstanding Female Performance in a Comedy Television Series category. Jake T. Austin was nominated in the male category. Selena was also nominated for a 2009 NAACP Image Award in the category of Outstanding Performance in a Youth/Children's Program for her role on *Wizards*.

Selena Gomez

that has a gym next door, where you can often find their parents exercising while the kids hit the books.

"Every Wednesday we get up and go to what is called a table read," Jennifer explains. "A table read is basically when everyone sits around a table and acts out that week's script to see how it flows. The rest of the day is spent doing school and rehearsing."

She continues, "Thursday and Friday, we rehearse more and the script gets tweaked so when we shoot, it can be at its best. On Monday, we shoot all the scenes that we can't shoot in front of the live studio audience. *Finally*, there is Tuesday. This is the day everyone waits for. Tuesday is tape night, the night when we have a live audience. It is exciting how the energy is

In "Fairytale," from the second season, Justin directs a school production of *Peter Pan* with Harper cast in the role of Tinker Bell. Alex, the understudy, steps in to play Tinker Bell, when Harper is sidelined by an injury. Fans were delighted to see Selena in her fetching Tinker Bell costume, not least because she sang "Fly to Your Heart" on the soundtrack for the Disney animated film *Tinker Bell*.

just different on tape days. The audience brings in such a grand feeling to the set."

Rehearsals and tapings may be followed by a publicity shoot or media interview before the work day concludes. You'd think the costars would tire of each other after spending so much time together, but they often hang out after-hours too. "We text each other as soon as we leave set," Selena says. "We ask our parents, 'Can we go to the mall? Can we go to the movies?' Our parents laugh at us because they're like, 'You act like you never see these people,' but they're like my family. I cried when the first season was over because my little brother was going back to New York, and my older brother was going to Utah to shoot *Dadnapped*. So we call each other every day, 'What are you doing? I miss you.'"

Being Alex

Rarely an episode goes by when Alex doesn't get herself into some kind of mess, often created by using magic for all the wrong reasons. The middle child and only daughter, she needs to constantly prove herself as a wizard, yet can't help getting sidetracked by familiar girl concerns, such as boys, clothes, and sibling rivalry.

Because there are so many special effects on *Wizards*, the actors often perform their scenes in front of a green screen. "The special effects can be a little difficult, but it is also a good challenge for me as an actress having to act like I am somewhere where I am not," Selena says. "The first time I had to talk to the green tape, I had to have one of my castmates read their lines off screen to me so I could get the feeling."

"The *quinceañera* episode was probably my favorite, or the episode where Alex wanted to go to a rated-R movie," Selena says. "She tries to put a spell on herself to magically go into the movie theater, but she ends up actually *in* the movie, so she's stuck in this scary movie sorority-house flick, and they shot it just like a movie. It was so much fun because it was like being able to shoot an actual scary movie."

In the *quinceañera* episode, Alex disappoints her mother by saying that she doesn't want to hold the traditional celebration of a girl's 15th birthday, which is similar to a sweet 16. Since her mom didn't have a *quinceañera* of her own, Alex casts a spell to swap bodies with her, and the party goes forward with a much more enthusiastic teenager.

Apparently, there isn't much Selena wouldn't do to get a laugh. She says, "I've had to pour chocolate all over myself. I've had mashed potatoes in my hair. We've 'flown' magic carpets. I get turned into a tiger in one episode! I think this show's all about the craziness, and we've done a lot of crazy stuff here."

She might be willing to get silly on set, but Selena and her young costars are still serious professionals. "I've worked with adults who are far more difficult than anybody in my cast right now," says *Wizards* executive producer Peter Murrieta. "I've seen Selena stand back by the doorway when they load the audience out at the end of the night, thanking everybody for coming. They are more gracious and professional and friendly than a lot of grownups I've worked with."

Love potions

"I think you see that our characters evolve," Selena hinted before the second season of *Wizards*. "You know, we're starting to deal with issues more mature and more our age, like Alex gets her first boyfriend. You see what every girl goes through on the first date — jitters, having a first kiss, having a fight with someone that you like. I think along that level it's how our characters are slowly maturing."

Throughout the series, the teenage trickster's best spells seem to come about when love is on the line, although not always with Alex's intended results . . .

- In "Justin's Little Sister," Alex drinks both halves of a love potion — and she falls in love with herself!
- In "Baby Cupid," Alex calls on Cupid to make her parents fall in love again after an argument over magic.
- In "The Supernatural," Alex tries to woo a boy named Riley (Brian Kubach) by making him think she's his baseball team's good luck charm.
- In "Alex's Spring Fling," Alex's boyfriend, Riley, dumps her, so she tries to save face by bringing an attractive mannequin to life.
- In "Racing," Alex helps her father restore an old car for a race in order to get closer to a hot-rodder named Dean (Daniel Samonas).
- In "Alex's Brother, Maximan," the Russo siblings have to work hard together after they fail a group project, which puts Alex's first real date with her new boyfriend, Dean, in jeopardy.
- In "Saving Wiz Tech," Alex falls hard for a boy named Ronald, only to discover that her crush is a kidnapper who must be stopped!
- In "Beware Wolf," it's Justin's turn for a fumbled romance when he falls for a werewolf who turns him into one too!
- In "First Kiss," Alex turns back time to give Justin another — and another, and another — attempt at a first kiss.
- In "Pop Me and We Both Go Down," Alex inflicts Justin with a large zit just before he takes a date to the junior prom.

Being a teenager can be tricky

Two *Wizards of Waverly Place* compilation DVDs offer favorite episodes and behind-the-scenes footage for fans who need a little magic to tide them over between seasons.

Wizards of Waverly Place: Wizard School includes four episodes from the first season, including the two-part mid-season episode "Wizard School," which sees Justin and Alex heading off to a summer academy called Wiz Tech. There they have the full "Hogwarts" experience, down to the robes and Harry Potter spectacles. Also included are the episodes "Curb Your Dragon" and "Disenchanted Evening," plus a tour of the set and special effects.

A second DVD volume, *Wizards of Waverly Place: Supernaturally Stylin'*, comes with the bonus feature "Fashionista Presto Chango!" — a peek at the show's wardrobe department and the cast's own fashion styles.

chapter 5
demi camps out

"I think that I won't ever relate to a character as much as I did Mitchie – going to school and feeling insecure and then finding herself through music . . . That's pretty much my life story!" – Demi

Demi's favorite colors are black and red.

As the Bell Rings introduced Demi to Disney viewers, but Selena had even bigger plans for her BFF. "I was absolutely determined to get her on the Disney Channel with me," she has said in interviews, meaning that Demi was ready for a show like Wizards of Waverly Place.

What followed was like a scene out of, well, a Disney movie. During a break in taping a Wizards episode, Selena beckoned Demi from her seat in the studio audience and invited her to entertain the crowd with a song. Demi wowed everyone — audience members and studio executives alike — with a rendition of Christina Aguilera's "Ain't No Other Man."

After her impromptu performance, "We realized [Demi] needed to be a larger part of our programming," says Gary Marsh, president of entertainment at the Disney Channel. Before long, the network had found the project that would take Demi from the hallways of As the Bell Rings to sharing the screen with the hottest act of 2008.

Camp Rock: The story

While many think of Camp Rock as a Jonas Brothers vehicle, their roles were actually added later. "It was always written as the girl's story: a Cinderella story of a girl who wants to go to camp, can't afford it," said Disney's Michael Healy, the senior vice-president of original movies. Once the boys were on board, however, the teleflick became one of the most anticipated events in the network's history.

Demi reportedly sang Aretha Franklin's "Ain't No Way" at her audition for Camp Rock, impressing casting directors just as she had those present for her surprise solo at the Wizards' studio. "We needed somebody who was a talented singer," Healy says, "and when Demi came in, she just was so radiant and such a great singing talent that we thought, 'How could we turn her down?'"

Demi was cast in the lead role as Mitchie Torres, an aspiring singer who can't afford the hefty fees at a special camp for young rock musicians until her mother (Maria Canals-Barrera) takes a job in the camp kitchen. Mitchie becomes friends with Caitlyn (Alyson Stoner) and strikes an uneasy friendship with Tess Tyler (Meaghan Jette Martin), head of the camp's popular girls' clique. Mitchie impulsively tells her new pals that her mom is president of Hot Tunes TV China, setting herself up for the constant worry that her lie will be exposed.

A bona fide rock star named Shane, played by Joe Jonas, arrives on the scene.

The lead singer of a hit band called Connect 3, Shane's success has turned him into an arrogant brat. His band mates, Jason (Kevin Jonas) and Nate (Nick Jonas), send him back to the camp where he got his start to remind him of his musical roots.

One night, Shane overhears Mitchie singing a beautiful song, but he doesn't see her face, and becomes obsessed with finding the girl with the striking voice. Meanwhile, Shane and Mitchie are becoming friends, and possibly more, until her lie is exposed, and Mitchie's summer of music and romance threatens to nosedive into the lake.

Demi's performance as Mitchie, an awkward and shy character who comes into her own, became a personal journey of sorts. "When I was filming in Canada, I really found out who I was," Demi says. "As I was doing the scene where I rock out on stage at the end, I evolved. It was really cool."

Not that Demi agrees with all of her character's decisions. "I don't like liars, and she tends to lie to have a good reputation," she says, "but it's innocent. Her intentions aren't mean, but she just gets caught up in the crowd there. I don't like that!"

The Jonas Brothers

When Demi auditioned for *Camp Rock*, she had no idea that the Jonas Brothers would be her costars. At the time, the boys were promising up-and-comers, soon to become massive stars.

Originally, Disney approached just one Jonas brother — Joe, for the lead male role

Joe Jonas Fun Facts

- Joseph Adam Jonas was born in 1989 in Casa Grande, Arizona.
- The second-oldest Jonas might look like leading man material, but to those closest to him, he's a clown. He considered going into comedy instead of music.
- Joe's favorite color is blue.
- He loves chicken cutlet sandwiches with mayo and his favorite dessert is chocolate marshmallow ice cream.
- Whose show would Joe line up to see? "I would go see the Spice Girls. I would stand in line for, like, three weeks. Or, like, an hour. I would totally love to go see that concert. I'm just sayin'."

— but he insisted on creating parts for his brothers. It wasn't hard to convince the network to bring all three onboard. The New Jersey boys have always been a strong unit, on and off the stage; moreover, younger brother, Nick, and older brother, Kevin, have their fair share of loyal fans.

The Jonas Brothers hail from Wyckoff, New Jersey. Their father Paul, an ordained minister, met their mother, Denise, at a church singing group. Music always filled the Jonas household and took hold of Nick very early. Nick was performing on

The boys considered calling their band Sons of Jonas before settling on the Jonas Brothers.

Broadway by age seven, appearing in *Les Misérables*, *Beauty and the Beast*, *A Christmas Carol: The Musical*, and *Annie Get Your Gun*. Joe caught the acting bug from his brother, landing a part in *La Bohème*.

Nick had early aspirations to launch a solo singing career. In 2002, he released a Christmas tune co-written with his father called "Joy to the World (A Christmas Prayer)," which attracted the interest of Columbia Records. When the label learned, in 2005, there was not one but three talented Jonas Brothers, the boys landed their first record deal.

Their debut album, *It's About Time*, was released in 2006. Disappointing sales led to Columbia dropping the boys in early 2007, but Disney's Hollywood Records quickly

"Camp Rock is all about standing up for yourself and finding your own style and being an individual and embracing your voice," Alyson Stoner says. "I think that every person can relate to that in their own way."

moved in. The band's self-titled second album, *Jonas Brothers*, was released in 2007, and their third, *A Little Bit Longer*, in 2008.

The Disney machine knew that promoting the band to its core audience — tween-age girls — would take a multi-pronged approach, and lots and lots of exposure. The boys guest-starred on *Hannah Montana* before joining Miley Cyrus on her Best of Both Worlds tour in

the fall of 2007. Appearances on *Dick Clark's New Year's Rockin' Eve, The Ellen DeGeneres Show, Dancing with the Stars*, and *American Idol* followed. They even sang from a White House balcony during the annual Easter Egg Roll!

The brothers' trademark harmony vocals have earned them a Grammy nomination for Best New Artist, and in 2008 they took home an American Music Award for on their Look Me in the Eyes tour throughout North America. Meanwhile, the Jonas Brothers were already on to the next big thing — summer 2008's sizzling Burnin' Up tour, which left them with barely enough time to catch their breath before beginning work on *J.O.N.A.S.*, a comedy series on the Disney Channel, which premiered in spring 2009.

All this, and *Camp Rock*.

Throughout this whirlwind of successes, the boys have stuck together, which has helped all three immensely. "People are kind of freaked out when we actually don't fight," says Kevin. "We actually do hang out and laugh together and joke around. We have a really good dynamic as three of us, and as a family, and as a team. It's pretty awesome."

The brothers have also managed to stay remarkably grounded. "It's definitely been extremely intimidating to work with people who are as known as 'The Jonas Brothers,'" Demi says. "But what I've learned is that the more people that you work with the more you realize they are just people. There have been times where I definitely made a fool of myself and embarrassed myself by getting too starstruck but it has kind of calmed down a little bit, but I definitely don't get sick of it."

Breakthrough Artist of the Year. From May to September 2008, the boys starred in the Disney Channel original series *Living the Dream*, a reality show that followed them

Alyson Stoner (Caitlyn Geller)

The level-headed Caitlyn Geller, an aspiring music producer, is played by Alyson Stoner. She describes her character as the "moral

In *Camp Rock*, Mitchie endures her share of bullying from the mean girls in the camp, which reflected the bullying Demi suffered in real life at school.

backbone" of the story, the one character who is true to herself from the outset. "Caitlyn knows what she wants from life, which I can relate to because I'm very goal-oriented," Alyson says. "Caitlyn is very ambitious and she knows where she wants to go in life, just like me. I focus on the future a lot more than short-term goals."

Funny and sarcastic, true to her friends and to herself, the character of Caitlyn actually underwent a lot of changes before the movie began shooting. "When I first read the script, my name used to be Lourdes," Alyson says. "I was supposed to be a gothic girl and I read it and I'm thinking, 'Oh my gosh, this is insane,' but they changed it to Caitlyn and made her who she is now. I couldn't stop laughing on set while I was saying my lines. I could not believe that they were making me say something like

that but it was really funny and it got a laugh so it's good."

Born in 1994, Alyson got her big break co-hosting Disney's Channel's *Mike's Super Short Show* from 2002 to 2006. She voices the role of Isabella Garcia-Shapiro in Disney Channel's animated series *Phineas and Ferb*, and has guest-starred on many hit shows, including *The Suite Life of Zack & Cody, That's So Raven!*, and Nickelodeon's *Drake and Josh*. Her film credits include *Cheaper by the Dozen, Cheaper by the Dozen 2*, and *Alice Upside Down*.

Meaghan Jette Martin (Tess Tyler)

Every camp has its inner circles. *Camp Rock*'s is performed by a trio of talented performers, whose real-life personalities couldn't be more different from their onscreen personalities. Tess Tyler is the clique's leader. She's

The cast of *Camp Rock* at the show's premiere. "I loved the script," says Maria Canals-Barrera, who plays Demi's mom. "It's another great parent role that is integral to the story, with her realizing and accepting and being happy about who she is and where she's at in life."

played to bossy perfection by Meaghan Jette Martin, who impresses with two solo songs in *Camp Rock*. Tess brings Mitchie into her tight circle only to compete with her for Shane's affection.

Naturally bubbly, friendly, and energetic, 16-year-old Meaghan had to shift gears when the cameras rolled. "The hardest part was to have to be mean to these people that I was getting so close to in the movie," says Meaghan, whose acting credits include

Disney Channel's *The Suite Life of Zack & Cody*, Nickelodeon's *Just Jordan*, and CBS's *Close to Home*. "We were all becoming best friends, and you know, the director would call, 'Action!' and I would have to yell at them. So that wasn't so much fun! But the entire cast was great, and I mean, they knew I was acting, so it was fun."

Alyson Stoner vividly remembers one such episode, a scene in which her character, Caitlyn, gets into an argument with

Meaghan's Tess. "She and I in real life are so close but we had to argue with each other and act like we didn't like each other so there's noodles that we get to throw at each other," she says. "It's very crazy and insane but in between takes, we'd actually give each other a hug and you know, let them know that it's nothing personal; it's only in the script."

Jasmine Richards (Peggy)

Jasmine Richards plays Peggy, one of Tess's sidekicks, a born follower who thankfully finds her own way by the end of the flick. She says, "I think my character is such a good role model for kids because it just proves that someone can do anything even if they're being held back by that one person who's slightly above them — like the mean girl or the popular girl from school. You can always just stand up and be yourself."

Born in 1990, in Scarborough, Ontario, Canada, Jasmine starred in the Disney Channel series *Naturally Sadie* and had supporting roles in the feature films *Devotion* and *Charlie Bartlett*. Like many of her costars, she has learned to juggle school and career, and the camp setting didn't get her off the hook for studying. "A lot of us had schoolwork to complete on the set," she says. "I'm Canadian, so I had to do two hours of schooling every day. You know what? It was really hard to balance school with *Camp Rock*. It was strange working away between scenes — but most of us had to do it. At least we all studied in the same room together."

Anna Maria Perez de Tagle (Ella)

The third "mean girl," Ella, is played by Anna Maria Perez de Tagle, a much gentler soul in real life. Of Ella she says: "She's not so smart, she's kind of a ditz, but her character changes completely towards the end of the movie. She's obsessed with makeup, hair, clothes, and lip gloss most of all. I talk about lip gloss 24/7 in the movie."

The 18-year-old had met Demi a few weeks earlier on the set of *Just Jordan*. "When I found out she got Mitchie, I called her and said 'Oh congrats,'" Anna Maria says. "Like a week later, she found out I got Ella and she called me and she's like 'Congrats, we're so excited!'"

In addition to a starring role on the CBS series *Cake*, Anna Maria has had a guest role on *Hanna Montana*, hosted Disney's *Sing-Along Bowl-Athon*, and was a junior singer finalist on CBS's *Star Search*.

On set

BOP Magazine posted an interview with Joe Jonas from the set on YouTube. The teen rag asked him to spill a secret about the film's production. "We're in [rural] Canada," he said, from the top-secret location in the Haliburton Highlands region of Ontario, far from the metropolitan city of Toronto. "There's really no cell service, or internet, or anything out here, so you really feel like you're at camp" — he smiled — "except that you get hair and makeup and catering."

While there were some creature comforts during the shoot, it was an intense schedule. When the going got rough, Demi called her stepfather. "I need him in the mornings and at night and for support," she says. "Some days it gets so stressful that I can be in tears. *Camp Rock* was my first movie, and in the first two weeks, I got really sick of exhaustion. I was in my trailer sweating. Drips of sweat were just coming off me because I was so stressed. It really does affect your health — how much you work, especially being this young. . . . But you get used to it. You can't always rely on your parents, too, when you're the one who has to do the

Back in the 1980s, *Camp Rock* composer Julie Brown was famous for her outrageous satires of the music industry's top stars, including Madonna and Sheena Easton. Her hilarious music videos got constant play on MTV, and she had big screen success with the 1988 comedy *Earth Girls Are Easy*, which she wrote and starred in. She played the gym teacher in *Clueless*, a role she returned to in the TV series by the same name. Julie Brown is now a familiar face on the E! Network, where she is a frequent commentator.

lines and you're the one who has to focus. They can't be doing the scene with me. But I need them 24/7."

Filming had its lighter moments, too. Sometimes there's nothing like a blooper to provide some much-needed comic relief. "There's one scene in the movie where it's supposed to be such a serious scene," costar Anna Maria remembers. Demi was "just crying to death, and Joe's supposed to be mad at her and yelling at her. And then he just kind of gets out of his character and forgets his lines, which makes Demi crack up, and makes everyone on set crack up. And it was the funniest scene ever."

Demi offers, "In rehearsals, Joe was dancing on stage and he didn't notice where

he was going. He completely dances off the stage and just falls. It's one of those moments that, every time I think about it, I just laugh."

The actors bonded during the long shoot, rehearsing, eating their meals together, and studying together. "Every person in *Camp Rock* was staying in the same hotel," Demi recalls. "The brothers would always hold a party in their room. They're like, 'Hey Demi! Dance party, my room, five minutes!' It was fun."

The movie was directed by Matthew Diamond, who is accustomed to the demands of guiding young performers and creating audience-pleasing dance numbers from his work on *That's So Raven!* and the reality TV show *So You Think You Can Dance.*

The music for *Camp Rock* was written by Julie Brown, along with Paul Brown, Regina Hicks, and Karen Gist. Demi sings three songs on the soundtrack, including a duet with Joe Jonas. Recording together was an emotional experience — it was when laying down the tracks for the movie that the enormity of the project suddenly hit Demi. "That was one of those moments where it was like, 'Wow, I get to do a duet with Joe Jonas and months before I was just jamming to their stuff!'" Demi says. "I listened to the playback of my song for the first time with him and I cried . . . I was like, 'Mom, that's Joe Jonas, you know?'"

It was a life-changing project, emotionally and physically draining, but in the end, Demi concluded that her experience with *Camp Rock* was one of the best she'd ever had. "I had a lot of fun and I learned a lot about myself too," she says, "because my character finds herself through music and really figures out who she is, and that is almost exactly what I was going through at the time."

Success!

A whopping 8.9 million total viewers tuned in when *Camp Rock* aired on the Disney Channel on June 27, 2008, and later on ABC's *The Wonderful World of Disney*, making it the second most-watched original movie on the network. *Variety Magazine* had predicted that "*Camp Rock* has a virtually impossible act to follow in *High School Musical 2*," but while it did fall short of *HSM2*'s 17 million viewers, it still impressed industry watchers.

Ecstatic fans rejoiced when Disney announced that *Camp Rock 2* would begin production in early 2009. Plans for the film have been kept hush-hush, so fans will have to content themselves with the DVD and Blu-ray editions of the *Camp Rock: Extended*

There are real rock camps where kids can learn to play instruments, compose music, and strut their stuff! Rock Star Camp in Toronto is coordinated by Tundra Music, a vintage guitar dealer and recording studio. In Portland, the Rock n' Roll Camp for Girls encourages girls to make some noise. "We've never been to a camp like Camp Rock," Kevin Jonas says, "but we wish we had."

Rock Star Edition, and the many product tie-ins that have appeared since the movie's release. "I was looking through the product book before anything came out, and there was a lawn chair and a lamp. I was like, 'All right, whatever,'" Demi says with a laugh.

Sales of the lawn chair may not be brisk, but fans have been scooping up the Mitchie and Shane action figures that sing songs from the soundtrack. (Demi admits that having a doll in her likeness is pretty strange, "especially when my friends tell me that they change her clothes. That's a little weird.") A novelization of the film, titled *Camp Rock: The Junior Novel*, and the *Camp Rock Second Session* series, has also been popular.

chapter 6
cinderella tale

"People probably didn't think I would get far because of where I'm from. . . . Being able to do what I've always wanted to do my entire life is a gift, and my whole dream has come true. To see where I am, from where I was, is just crazy." – Selena

Soon after the first episodes of *Wizards of Waverly Place* began airing in fall 2007, Selena was hard at work on the follow-up to Hilary Duff's 2004 flick *A Cinderella Story*. Selena played the lead character in the direct-to-DVD movie, which was released in September 2008. (It also aired on ABC Family in January 2009.) "It's basically our updated version of the Cinderella story," Selena says, "so I drop an MP3 player instead of a glass slipper and he's got to find me through music."

Selena has described the experience of filming her first lead role as "nerve-wracking," but Drew Seeley, who plays her modern-day Prince Charming, claims she handled it with grace. "She's this really down-to-earth person," he says. "She doesn't take herself too seriously and neither do I. So we got off on the right foot and started joking at the auditions, right before we started reading."

Cinderella wears Converse

Another Cinderella Story is about a talented teen named Mary, daughter of a backup singer to the former pop star Dominique Blatt, who took Mary in after her father passed away. Jane Lynch delivers a side-splitting portrayal of the aging singer, who has been reduced to doing commercials for back acne cream. In the tradition of all Cinderellas, Mary cleans Blatt's house to earn her keep and suffers much verbal abuse for her efforts. Mary sneaks off to a high school dance, where she performs an electric tango with Joey Parker (Andrew "Drew" Seeley), a teen idol who is taking a break from the high life to finish his senior year among the ordinary folk.

"The idea essentially was to take the Cinderella fable and retell it," the film's director, Damon Santostefano, says. "In doing that, it very much turned out to be not so much a sequel of *A Cinderella Story*, but rather a completely new retelling of a modern day extrapolation of the fable. On top of that, it's a dance musical so it's really the comedy dance musical version of the Cinderella fable."

Selena explained to MTV that a dancing Cinderella puts a unique "spin" on the story. "I think that brings a whole new element to the movie. She's an aspiring dancer, and she wants to go after her dreams. She sings as well. It's her achieving her dreams in a different way."

But adding "professional dancer" to your resumé takes more than a wave of a magic wand. "I took two months of dance training," Selena says. "I was trying to act like I'd been a dancer my entire life . . . It was a challenge, but now I'm addicted to dancing. I love it."

Drew had a leg up on Selena. With years of dancing behind him, he made sweeping his costar off her feet — literally — look effortless. "The first things I did before singing and acting, my parents got me into ballet, tap, jazz, all that kind of stuff," Drew says. "From [ages] eight to thirteen, four or five days a week, that's all I did."

Another Cinderella Story is set in the summertime in Beverly Hills but was shot in chilly Vancouver. To ensure that Selena and Drew's breath didn't show up on screen, they had to suck on ice cubes between takes and were warmed with heaters.

The Ottawa-born actor somehow found the time to develop his singing and composing skills as well. In 2006, he scored a hit with the super-catchy, rhythm-driven "Get 'Cha Head in the Game," which he co-wrote and sung on the first *High School Musical* soundtrack. It was nominated for the Emmy Award in the Best Original Song and Lyrics category. Drew toured with the original *HSM* cast in the live *High School Musical: The Concert*, taking over the lead role Troy from Zac Efron, who was busy filming the flick *Hairspray*. Drew's voice had replaced Zac's on the movie's soundtrack, as well. Although Zac is in fact a fine singer whose own voice appears on the subsequent *HSM* soundtracks, the confusion made him uncomfortable and he cleared things up

Selena with Zac Efron at the *Teen Vogue* Young Hollywood party.

car, which I don't know how to do," he recalls. "That was kind of embarrassing because I had to stop a millimeter from the camera, and I could not get it right, so we ended up having about ten crew guys push us into frame and stop me right at the right time. Selena got a kick out of that too. I was usually the butt of most of the jokes."

The dance partners became fast friends on the shoot, although they disagree about which scene is the very best of the film. Selena's favorite musical number was the tango piece. "It's when the two characters meet and fall in love. It's one of the hardest dances I've learned, but the most beautiful."

Drew, on the other hand, loves the big concert scene at the end of the movie. "We had two hundred extra people in there, a full crowd, and we got to do the dance and the songs full out with a band and dancers and the lights going and everything and the

Selena's first onscreen kiss was a brief smooch with Dylan Sprouse on *The Suite Life of Zack & Cody*. "That was fun," Selena dished to *Girl's Life* magazine. "He was shorter than me, so I had to bend down a little bit." At the time of the interview, Selena was shooting *Another Cinderella Story* with Drew Seeley. "Drew is definitely taller, so I think this one will go a little smoother," she predicted. It did.

through the media. "I didn't even sing on the first album. It wasn't my voice in the movie," Zac told *Rolling Stone*. "I felt extremely guilty."

Drew may have come to *Another Cinderella Story* with dance experience under his belt, but the *Cinderella* shoot was not without its challenges for the 26-year-old performer. "I had to drive a stick shift

fog machine," he says. "It was just really exciting. It really felt like a real concert, and we got to live inside of that for about a week, so that was my favorite part."

Triple threats

Selena, Demi, and Drew can sing, act, *and* dance! In the entertainment business, a performer with this trio of talents is known as a "triple threat." Some stars, such as Rihanna and Lindsay Lohan, haven't stopped there. In addition to their success in music and film, both have made forays into fashion. Can we expect Demi and Selena to strut their own designs on the catwalk in years to come?

You can probably count Selena out of the fashion business. She may have played the belle of the ball, but she's never been one for haute couture. At the 2008 Teen Choice Awards, Selena shrugged off reporters' praise for her blue strapless mini dress. "When people talk about my style, I'm like, 'What style?'" she said. "I'm just a jeans, T-shirt, flip-flops, and hat kind of girl."

Selena can cook!
Selena's special dish is chicken
with Hawaiian teriyaki sauce.

Q: Which triple threat's break-through role was playing Selena's namesake?
A: Jennifer Lopez

Selena's love of Converse sneakers is well known — she has admitted to owning at least 20 pairs. "I remember one time I went to the store and this girl goes — I heard her behind me — she says, 'Oh my gosh! Is that Selena Gomez?' . . . And then a girl next to her goes, 'No, trust me. That's not her. She wouldn't dress like that.'"

House rules

Cinderella's stepmom could be harsh, to say the least. Selena's parents are a little more laidback, although they expect their rules to be followed. That means home by curfew — usually 11:30 — and pitching in around the house. "She has to do her own laundry," Selena's mother has said. "If she cooks, I clean. If I cook, she cleans. She has to help feed the dogs."

As for those glitzy but chaotic red carpet events, Selena's mom says, "She never goes to movie premieres, wrap parties, or anything related to the business without a parent. Period. That rule is not changing until she is 21!"

"Selena knows the words to every single one of my songs – even the songs I just started writing! She's my biggest fan and she's so awesome." – Demi

> "There's a song
> [on **Don't Forget**] called
> 'Believe' – it's pretty pop,
> but it means a lot to me,
> and I can relate to it a lot,
> just because I wrote it
> about feeling insecure, just
> wanting to feel beautiful."

Music has been an integral part of Demi's life since she was very young. "My dad bought me a guitar when I was eight," she says. "I didn't have a desire to play it and he was just like, 'Well, whenever you need it, it's there.' I'm like, alright, whatever, I'm probably never gonna play it.' And then, I don't know . . . one day I got really lonely and I had already started piano and I told my dad, I really want to play guitar. So I started focusing on piano and guitar quite a bit and I would take lessons up to two or three times a week."

Music became Demi's comfort, inspiration, and means of self-expression. It's also a powerful part of Disney's marketing strategy, which promotes shows and movies through albums released by its record label, Hollywood Records. Few Disney stars are merely actors these days; most are actor-singers (or singer-actors). After *Camp Rock* wrapped, no time was wasted taking Demi's music career to the next level.

Burnin' Up tour

During the summer of 2008, the Jonas Brothers embarked on a tour called Burnin' Up to promote their third album, *A Little Bit Longer*. They brought Demi along as their opening act, giving her the same invaluable exposure they'd received when touring with Miley Cyrus.

Demi prepared for her concert dates with the JoBros by doing a small tour on her own, which included stops in her home state of Texas. The pre-tour "taught me how to stay intact with the audience and not panic, how to handle mistakes and things like that. I've dropped the microphone several times," Demi told the *Houston Chronicle* in June 2008. She sounded confident when she added, "The fans in each city just keep growing and getting better."

Yet, Demi had a bad case of stage fright when the Burnin' Up tour kicked off on July 4, 2008, in Toronto. "I was so nervous the first time I ever went in front of a large crowd in Toronto," Demi remembers. "I was so nervous and I was crying and Selena was there, my best friend, and she was like, 'Are you sure you're not nervous?' and I was like, 'No, no, no — I've got it' and then all of a sudden I was like, 'Now I'm really nervous and I don't know what to do, I'm scared' and she was like, 'Oh my gosh, you've got to pull it together. You've got it, so don't worry about it.' So that was pretty funny."

During the tour, Demi experienced the highest and lowest points in her life. Sharing the spotlight with the Jonas

Demi's favorite band is Paramore and her favorite songs are "Sugar Skulls" and "Almost Four" by Wolftron.

mom was home with my sisters and I was with my stepdad the entire tour. We built up a friendship that is priceless."

The more experienced Jonas Brothers were a reliable source of support, not only throughout the tour, but as Demi's music career continued to hurtle forward. "They're very classy," Demi says. "You don't find many teenage guys who are so classy anymore, old-fashioned. They're rock stars so you really don't expect it. They really surprise you to see how nice, intelligent, and professional they are."

She recalls: "When I needed a ride home because it was pouring down with rain, I was just going to walk to the hotel room — it was, like, twenty feet away — but they wanted to make sure that I got there. They said, 'No, it's nighttime and you shouldn't go out in the rain anyway, so we'll drive you in our golf cart.' It was just very thoughtful, they were raised very well."

Both the performers and fans have many mementoes to remind them of the tour highlights. Demi appears in the book *Burnin' Up: On Tour with the Jonas Brothers*, a collection of photographs taken throughout the tour (including polaroids by Joe Jonas), which offers an intimate look at life on the road. Demi is also featured in Walt Disney Pictures' *Jonas Brothers: The 3D Concert Experience* released in February 2009. The concert and behind-the-scenes documentary footage is similar to the 2008 release *Hannah Montana & Miley Cyrus: Best of*

Brothers was an obvious thrill for the teenager, but the late nights, constant travel, and pressure to please the large crowds took its toll. "The lowest [point] was being apart from my family on tour. I basically started doing press things in January and I went home for probably a total of a week from then through August," she says. "My

Demi opens for the Jonas Brothers in Pittsburgh during their Burnin' Up tour. "There's a microphone on the side of the stage that we use to tell people if we need water or we need something, and it's called a talkback mike," Demi said during the tour. "Only we, the performers, can hear it in our earpieces. And there are times when the Jonas Brothers will use the mike to try to mess me up while I'm singing . . . I've laughed in the middle of a song!"

Both Worlds Concert. It includes guest performances by songstress Taylor Swift, Joe's former girlfriend.

In the recording studio

"Whenever I write music, it's never planned," Demi says. "I'm always either playing guitar or piano first, and then I'll write lyrics to it. But I love writing lyrics about experiences that I've had in my life."

When songwriting, Demi often includes references to "little things, like things you do every day. Like in one of the songs it talks about your fingertips on a window, it's something everyone does but doesn't really pay attention to. And that could be about coping with everyday life or it could be about how I miss you, you know? And I like to pull from past experiences."

Demi drew heavily on her own experiences when she headed to the recording studio to create her first album, *Don't Forget*, co-writing all but two of the eleven songs. The album was a joint effort, written and recorded with the help of the Jonas Brothers on a break from the tour. "I went to go visit them for maybe two weeks on tour and we basically just wrote and we had so much fun," Demi says.

The boys co-wrote six tracks, among them the title song, "Don't Forget," which is very meaningful to Demi. The lyrics describe "a personal experience that hap-

Demi's musical co-writer, Robert Schwartzman, comes from a very famous family. He is the lead singer of the rock band Rooney. His brother is the actor Jason Schwartzman, who has appeared in movies such as *Rushmore*, *Marie Antoinette*, and *The Darjeeling Limited*, and is also a musician. Robert's uncle is the legendary director Francis Ford Coppola, and the director Sofia Coppola is his cousin. His other cousin is actor Nicolas Cage, from *National Treasure*. Reunions must be interesting in that family!

pened where I was really into somebody and they basically walked away." The words "don't forget" also describe Demi's desire to remember the experience of recording her first album, which includes a duet with Joe Jonas called, "On the Line."

The album was produced by John Fields, the talent behind *A Little Bit Longer* and *Jonas Brothers*. It balances pop music that is age-appropriate for Demi's young fans with her love for an edgier brand of music. "Kelly Clarkson, when she first went rock, was totally my inspiration," Lovato says. "I decided to try it and it was like, 'Wow, this fits more.'" She hastens to add, "I

The video for *Don't Forget*'s first single, "Get Back," was shot in Brooklyn under the Manhattan Bridge. Shooting started around 5 p.m. and continued all night long. "I like working at night," Demi says. Her mother has always said Demi is "nocturnal," although "lots of coffee" was necessary to get through the shoot.

realize, though, that I am a pop singer. And I'm not gonna try to be too 'Oh, I'm hard-core, I'm a rock girl.' No, I'm with the Disney Channel! But bubblegum isn't really my thing."

She adds, "I didn't really get to channel any hard rock, but the song I wrote with Robert Schwartzman — I wanted to write it like a song that had a southern rock feel, more rock than some of the songs on my album." Called "Party," the song is about "just having a good time."

Don't Forget was released in September 2008, debuting at number two on the Billboard 200. Not too shabby for an album largely recorded in ten days!

Metalhead

Much to the amusement of rock journalists, Demi — product of Disney's squeaky-clean teen idol machine — *loves* heavy metal. "I guess it started in school," she says. "I started listening to stuff with screaming in it, and then I started [exploring] more metal. MySpace helped me a lot, and friends will tell me about certain bands. And some of the bands I like aren't necessarily too metal. It's funny, because the Jonas Brothers dance and play dance music in their dressing room, and I'll be across the hall, and I just blare metal. People walk by and go, 'Really?'"

Demi has said she'd jump at the chance to collaborate with an existing band, such as Underoath, although she might not attach her name to the work. She says, "I

"I feel a lot of pressure when my voice is tired," Demi admitted. "Like one day, right before I went on *Good Morning America*, I completely lost my voice and I had a lot of stage fright actually. But I kinda pulled it off I guess, but my voice was still really tired."

Demi claims she has found the best treatment, which she always keeps backstage. "I have to have potato chips," she says. "The grease and the oil help your throat."

wish I could just secretly do vocals, and nobody would know it's me. I would love to just do a couple of screams. One time I was at soundcheck and I told my musical director that I really want to pig squeal, and he said, 'Go ahead — I don't care.' I didn't want to, because I could see there were fans nearby, and he said, 'Just do it.' And I did, and these fans reacted. They were like, 'Wow, that's awesome — I don't even know what that is, but it's cool.'"

On Demi's 16th birthday, she was delighted by a "shout out" video compiled by friends in which people sent their good wishes, including two of her rock idols. "Tommy Lee and Nikki Sixx wished me happy birthday," she says. "And I cried . . . I was like, 'Oh my gosh this is the coolest thing ever'! It was incredible."

chapter 8
living in la la land

"I think it's important to be careful of what you do and say and who you hang out with. Represent yourself well, even in the clothes you wear."
– Selena

Magazine covers, talk shows, public appearances, red carpets — all in a day's work when you're a teen superstar. But the reality of celebrity life can be much darker than the glossy pictures portray. "Just because you're on the Disney Channel and you always have a smile on your face, they think you're perfect," Demi says, "and it's obvious that nobody's life really is."

It's hard enough getting bullied in school; what happens when the entire world seems ready to pounce on your every misstep, when there are cameras waiting for you around every corner?

From costars to "frenemies"

As their fame spread, Demi and Selena started posting YouTube videos to keep in touch with fans. "Selena and I were noticing how hard it can be to write messages and comments to every single fan that you have," Demi says. "On YouTube, even

Selena messages her friends on her computer. Despite the media circus that erupted when Miley Cyrus and her friend Mandy posted a parody YouTube video of one that Selena and Demi had done, the girls said it was meant to be a joke and they were all friends.

though you're not speaking to them personally, you can at least say 'Hey, this is what I'm doing,' and you're getting to reach out to all of them. So, we made a video and all of a sudden it became this huge thing that other people were doing, too."

Each vlog shows Demi and Selena sitting in front of a webcam, up close and personal, while chatting about what's going on in their lives and just horsing around. Friends like the Jonas Brothers make guest appearances. Selena told radio host Ryan Seacrest, "We just want to show kids that we're probably the biggest nerds out there. . . .We just want to show that we're normal and like to do silly things."

The girls were bowled over by the response they received from fans. Millions of viewers watch Demi and Selena's videos, making them one of the hottest destinations on YouTube.

Many of those viewers were shocked when Miley Cyrus and her friend Mandy Jiroux posted a video of their own that parodied one of Demi and Selena's YouTube missives. In the original video, Demi and Selena chitchat about Demi's makeup, Selena's Power Rangers T-shirts, among other ordinary girl stuff. Miley and Mandy use the same language and show off their T-shirts and joke about a pretend gap marked on Mandy's teeth, while frequently dissolving into laughter. A notice appears at the end of the parody, stating "Check out our friends' YouTube!!!!! XOXOXO M & M."

Miley claims the spoof was just a silly

Selena meets with her fans before appearing on CBS's *The Early Show.*

joke and has said she's "super sorry" if the girls were offended. She told *Popstar! Magazine*: "We were just having fun . . . They have a YouTube account, and so at the end of our video we did put 'Go to their YouTube' . . . We were kind of supporting their channel, but also being silly because they were being funny, and that's our thing — to be funny." She added, "Elvis says, 'Imitation is the greatest form of flattery,' so we were imitating them being funny."

The resulting media storm took months to blow over, despite Miley's apology. Selena and Demi knew Miley, and said they took the video to be exactly what Miley said it was — just having fun. Selena tried to be Zen about it. "Dealing with the press is something that you've gotta start getting used to," she told *MTV News*, "and you know people want something to talk about, so they're going to have the two Disney girls — or three Disney girls — kind of feuding. "There's no feud — there's nothing to feud about, so why start a fight?" she continued. "It's something that we all have to live with, and unfortunately it involves friends."

Demi also brushed off the gossip, even joked about it. "I really don't know Miley that well. We didn't take offense or think it was a negative or a positive. It was just like, 'Okay, cool, Hannah Montana knows who I am'!"

Life in the limelight

"I can still go to the mall and totally not be recognized," Demi said cheerfully to Musiqtone.com. "Even when I dress up or whatever, and I'm wearing heels because I have an appearance right after, I don't get recognized unless I'm like with the boys, or with Selena or someone who is also known. I kinda like it though because I get to still live a normal life."

Not long after she made those remarks, Demi's career exploded. After her car was swarmed by paparazzi for the first time, Demi told *Access Hollywood*, "It's still surreal to me." She added, "I kinda got

nervous and a little claustrophobic."

Photographers and screaming fans have since become the stuff of everyday life. "It's been a tornado," Demi's mother says of her daughter's shoot to superstardom. "A Texas twister."

Rumors swirled around the web after Demi was photographed attending Miley Cyrus's sweet 16 party with marks on her wrists. Her press representative was compelled to issue a statement to *E! News* denying speculation that Demi is a self-mutilator, someone who compulsively cuts herself. "Demi was wearing gummy bracelets just prior to her appearance on the red carpet," publicist Allison Leslie explained, "Because of how tight they were, they left indentations on her wrist."

Fortunately for Demi, she has a BFF who knows exactly how she feels. "I think that it's so nice to go through all of this with someone that I love and that I care about and that I can trust," Selena says. "Because we're 16-year-old girls dealing with things, like being afraid to go outside [because of the paparazzi]. Things that are ridiculous. Our lives have changed since I've known her, since I was seven. It's just nice to have that support because it's very hard to come out to L.A. . . . and not know anybody and not be able to trust anybody."

Many stars complain about the constant presence of photographers, but Selena acknowledges that there's give and take between celebrities and paparazzi. Frequent public appearances feed fans' insatiable

Demi appeared with the Jonas Brothers and Miley Cyrus to play a benefit concert for the City of Hope Cancer Center in Los Angeles. The concert raised $1.2 million for cancer research and treatment programs.

appetite for photos, updates, and glimpses of their favorite celebs' everyday lives. Check a fan blog any day of the week, and there will almost certainly be a picture of Demi or Selena, whether attending a charity event or taking out the recycling. But with increased visibility comes decreased privacy. "There are both positive and nega-tive sides with having the paparazzi after you, but it keeps me in the limelight," Selena said. "I have to be nice to them, if I want them to be nice to me. It's something I have to get used to. A lot of celebrities want the paparazzi after them, so I'm not complaining!"

Selena credits her mother with keeping

To help encourage their fans to recycle, several Disney stars spent a day in February 2008 planting trees, recycling, and sharing a no-waste lunch. Maiara Walsh (*Cory in the House*), Emily Osment, Mitchel Musso, and Selena carried potted trees to areas that were in need of reforestation.

her feet on solid ground: "Before we got to California, she told me, 'You're going to hear the word yes a lot. You're this. You're that. Yes-yes-yes. So I'm the one who's going to tell you no — only because I love who you are now, and I don't want you to change.'"

And if living in La La Land starts going to Selena's head? "They'll take me right back to Texas and they will show me where I came from."

Demi performed at the 2008 Annual Arthur Ashe Kids' Day concert. Arthur Ashe was a tennis player who died in 1993, and he is remembered for his work with young people. A portion of the proceeds from the day's concert were given to the National Junior Tennis League, an organization that was founded by Ashe to help inner city children through sports.

Role models

Disney stars have a big responsibility to always put their best foot forward. With the media watching their every move, they must be careful to set a good example — on stage, on screen, and in their personal lives. As if being a teenager isn't hard enough!

"I'm glad that my job is to be a role model," Selena says. "But, at the same time, we're all 16-year-olds and we're going to make mistakes. I'm going to try my hardest to make those mistakes to myself and not let it interfere with my connection to my fans whatsoever."

At 15, on the set of a *Seventeen* magazine shoot, Selena announced to *Extra* that she planned to abstain from sex until marriage, telling the entertainment show that she has a reminder of that vow in the form of a promise ring. "I said, 'Dad, I want a promise ring.' He went to the church and got it blessed. He actually used me as an example for other kids," she said.

Miley Cyrus and all of the Jonas Brothers wear promise rings, also known as purity rings, and have publicly stated their decision to practice abstinence. "I'm going to keep my promise to myself, to my family, and to God," Selena says.

"Hilary Duff has stayed a really good role model," says Demi, who also has a promise ring, inscribed with the words "True Love Waits." (She wears it on a necklace.) "I mean, I'm sure she made mistakes, but you never saw them. I think it's really cool that someone can grow up and continue to be looked up to by young girls."

Demi has earned accolades for her strong anti-bullying stance, but her best friend isn't exactly sitting on her hands. Before the presidential election of November 2008, Selena took part in the UR Votes Count! campaign. "I'm very excited to be supporting it," she said. "It's basically educating teens on why it's important to vote and what's going on in the nation and what's going on in the world."

Why get involved in an election before she is old enough to vote herself? "It's wonderful that I am able to try to spread good out there," Selena says. "I want to make sure there is good press out there and make sure I can use my voice like I said. I think that maybe the younger kids might not get this, but since they look up to me they might get into it, which I think is adorable. I've actually had ten-year-olds come up to me saying that her and her older sister were learning about it. There's a ten-year-old learning about presidential issues."

Selena has big plans for expanding her charitable and advocacy work. She says: "My family and I want to start our own organization to work on global warming and a couple of other things. It's kind of sad when you walk up to teens nowadays and you start talking about global warming, and half of them say, 'What?' I want to educate everyone about that situation. Also, we just recently visited the Children's Hospital of Orange County and I want to do more with them. And for pets also, we want to do something for abused pets. We just want to do as much as possible. We recycle, we do everyday little things that people don't think will matter. But in reality, those little things are the most important. Doing everything you can do and spreading the word."

Being the public face of a charity is one way to make change, but Selena points out how effectively art can be used to promote ideas. "Music is powerful in a way that you can use your lyrics to get a message

Selena makes an appearance for UR Votes Count! in California, which shows people who are not old enough to vote that their voice still matters. People aged 13 to 17 are encouraged to vote at the UR Votes Count! kiosks in malls, and the results are posted to show how the younger demographic would have voted if they could.

Four-year-old Demi with her dad.

Following his divorce from Demi's mother, Patrick Lovato didn't see much of his daughter. Not only was he living far away in New Mexico, he was battling cancer. But that all changed in February 2008. After more than four years of separation, Demi used a rare break from work to surprise her father with a reunion. In an exclusive interview, Patrick told *Star* magazine, "I was at my dad's house when I heard a knock on the door, and he yelled out that someone wanted to see me. I walked out of the bedroom — and there was Demi! I couldn't believe how beautiful she was. The first thing she said to me was, 'Hey, partner . . . I love you!' We threw our arms around each other and began to cry."

The word "partner" was especially meaningful to Demi's dad, as father and daughter have long called each other by the pet name. "She'll always be 'my partner,'" said the proud father. "We have a special relationship that'll never change, no matter how big she becomes."

through, whether it's about an issue that's going on in the world or issues with yourself," Selena says, adding that acting can do the same. "One of my favorite movies is *Crash*. That movie sends an incredible message out and I wanted to make sure that all of my friends watched that movie."

Selena was also the face of the 2008 UNICEF Halloween campaign. The annual collection of spare change by trick-or-treaters has raised more than $140 million since it began in 1950. "I want to help encourage other kids to make a difference in the world," she says.

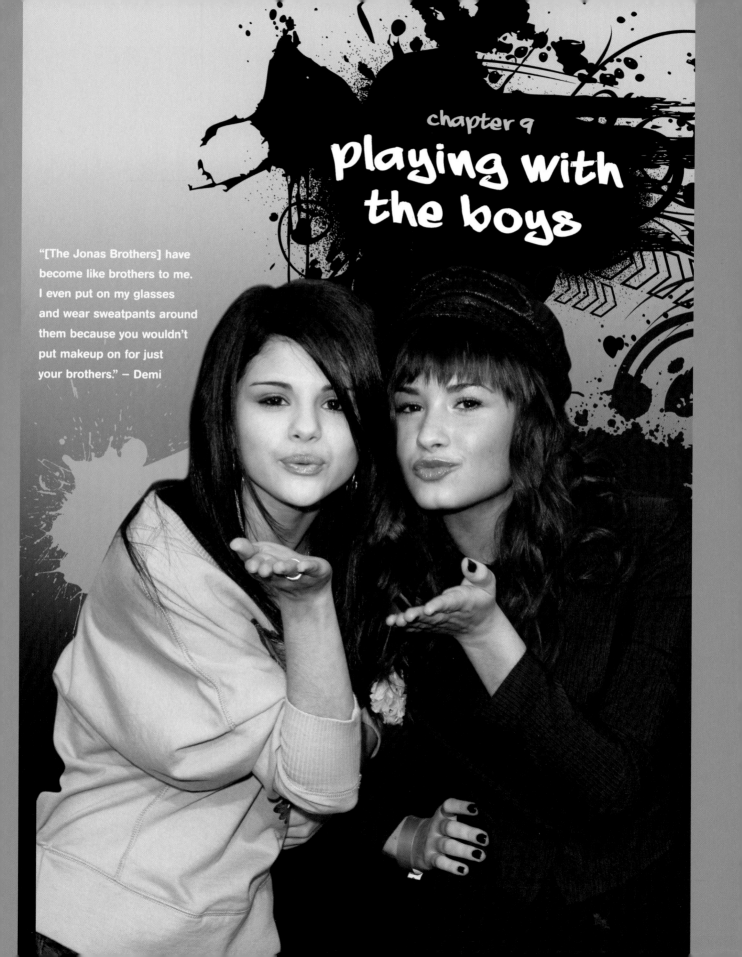

playing with the boys

"[The Jonas Brothers] have become like brothers to me. I even put on my glasses and wear sweatpants around them because you wouldn't put makeup on for just your brothers." – Demi

In the months leading up to the release of *Camp Rock*, fansites were full of gossip about rumored onscreen (and off-screen) kisses between Demi and Joe. "I've never kissed a Jonas brother, period," Demi stated for the record in *Seventeen*. "That would be kind of weird. Even in *Camp Rock*, Joe and I never kissed."

Competing over parts may be inevitable when your bestie happens to be in the same biz, but what about competing over boys? Surrounded by cute Disney costars, attending industry soirees with the fabulously famous, surely Demi and Selena occasionally set their sights on the same cute guy? "We actually have very different taste in boys," Selena insists. "I never really go for her type and she never goes for mine. We've never actually had that conflict. Even if that does happen to come up, we would just discuss it, but I don't really think we'll ever have that problem."

Demi may not have to vie with Selena for male attention, but there are millions of girls who are insanely jealous of her close proximity to those dreamy Jonas Brothers. "Imagine being new to Disney, and your first big job is being the romantic interest of one of the biggest heartthrobs on the channel," Demi told *Entertainment Weekly*. "Any girl that is a friend of the Jonas Brothers gets hate mail and is automatically suspected as a girlfriend."

Despite many a rumor to the contrary, Demi strongly denies that she ever dated Joe or any Jonas. "Joe and I never dated. We're really good friends," she says. "I just think it's funny that people try to pin me to

**Selena can spit
her gum high in the air
and catch it in her mouth
many times in a row.**

them. It's like, 'Oh, come on!' I think [if I were going to] I would have dated one of them by now!"

Still, Demi and the J-boys have been tight since their *Camp Rock* days, and touring together strengthened that bond. "I can definitely call Joe a best friend," Demi says. "On one of the first nights of filming *Camp Rock*, we sat there and spilled everything, and I talked about how I was bullied in school when I was younger. It was emotional, but it brought us close. I'm able to go to all of them with my problems."

Nick or not?

Selena's romantic entanglements are much harder to unravel. Although she shares a lot with her fans, she doesn't kiss and tell.

"Of course, boys are on every girl's mind. But I am only 15. I don't think I need a boyfriend right now. I have crushes and I go on dates . . . but younger kids my age take that stuff way too seriously." That was Selena in spring 2008.

By the summertime, rumors about Selena and Nick Jonas began to heat up when the media compared stories they'd shared about first kisses. Nick told *Girls' Life* magazine, "On one date, the girl said to me, 'I don't kiss on the first date.' So I said, 'I don't follow the rules.' Ooooh! It was so good!"

Compare that to Selena's account in *TWIST* of a very memorable smooch: "While we were slow dancing, my crush and I had our first kiss," she said. "I said, 'I don't kiss on the first date.' Then he said, 'Well, I never really play by the rules.'"

Coincidence? And if they *were* talking about the same special kiss, did they want fans to figure it out?

Selena played coy with a reporter from *Entertainment Weekly* when asked about whether she was involved with a Jonas brother. "They're really great guys," she said giggling. "I'm not confirming, but I'm not denying."

Soon after, *Rolling Stone* published a photograph of Selena and Nick taken during the Burnin' Up tour. They had their arms around each other, sharing an intimate moment just moments before he went on stage. The magazine noted that the Jonas Brothers' publicist hadn't wanted the photo to be made public.

Selena added fuel to the fire when she told *TWIST* that her favorite song among those she has written is "I'm Sorry," which is about "a boy I kind of fell for, but he couldn't let his ex-girlfriend go, and it was really difficult."

Selena with Daniel Samonas, her onscreen boyfriend in *Wizards of Waverly Place*.

their relationship, "7 Things." Had Nick inspired *two* songs — one by his ex-girlfriend and one by his current?

Selena quickly clarified in *People*, "It's definitely not about Nick Jonas," adding, "It's about someone back home in Texas. When I read it, I was like, 'Oh no, this gossip has to go away!' I haven't known the Jonas Brothers for that long, but I've gotten really close with all of them."

While Nick and Selena still haven't confirmed whether they are a couple, insiders definitely say it's on!

More recently, however, Selena has been seen with her onscreen boyfriend Daniel Samonas, who appears on *Wizards of Waverly Place* as Alex's boyfriend Dean. Could they be a couple off-screen, too?

Life mimics art

One romantic rumor has turned out to be true: Demi confirmed that she dated

She continued, "The song is basically me saying that I'm sorry that it didn't work out or that she used to be who she was. . . . But you have to let me in and you have to know that I'll do everything I can to make you happy and be the best I can be."

Not surprisingly, fans went wild. After all, Nick Jonas used to date Miley Cyrus, who had written a song of her own about

Hannah Montana star Cody Linley. "It's really weird because Cody's like the complete opposite of what I would normally be attracted to!" she says. "It's just because I've known him for so long that I've known the real side of him." She adds, "Normally, I go for the tight pants, the whole all black . . . I love rock stars. The bad boys, the bands."

It was a curious case of life imitating art, as Selena's *Hannah Montana* character had a crush on Cody Linley's character, once upon a time. But the relationship was put on hold, at least for now. "Right before [the Burnin' Up tour] we went on a date and talked a little bit and we decided that we should probably wait until I get back, which is totally fine, I need to focus. But he'll always be really special to me. He's a great guy!"

She may have been a little more upset than she let on. After the relationship was over, Selena says, "Demi came to me and she was really hurt. . . . We vent to each other, and then we make a video of the two of us venting it all out. Then, when we go back and watch the video, we just start laughing! We realize how much we overanalyzed the situation."

Demi confirmed that she did date *Hannah Montana*'s Cody Linley at one time.

chapter 10
demi & selena
–everywhere!

"There are always going to be pressures but if you have good people around you, it makes it easier to handle." – Demi

Most teens are experts at enjoying their downtime, whether they're hanging out at the mall, reading, playing basketball, or just lazing around. Not Demi and Selena. It seems whenever they have a moment to spare, a new project comes along to fill the slot!

In 2008, Selena costarred in her first feature film — although she didn't appear on camera. "I had never done animation, so I thought it would be cool to try something different," she says of *Horton Hears a Who*, which was released in 2008.

As the voice of Horton, Jim Carrey headed up an all-star cast that also included Will Arnett, Samantha Droke, Isla Fisher, Josh Flitter, Dan Fogler, Jonah Hill, Joey King, Laura Ortiz, Amy Poehler, Jaime Pressly, Seth Rogen, and Steve Carell as the Mayor of Whoville.

Selena was the voice of the Mayor of Whoville's daughters — all 90 of them. The then-15-year-old had to flex her acting muscles. "I had to change up my voice to do higher voices, and then bring it down to do lower voices. All of the Mayor's daughters look different, so I play many different characters."

Selena is a big basketball fan, and used to play on a team when she went to public school. Her favorite professional team is the San Antonio Spurs.

During some downtime while taping *Wizards of Waverly Place,* Selena skateboards behind the studio.

Unfortunately, Selena and Steve Carell recorded their parts separately, and never met. "It was kind of a bummer!" she said. "But at the same time, it was cool. I can see him and say, 'Hey, I played your daughter!'"

Demi and Selena ham it up (pun intended) with Miss Piggy when Selena hosted a show with the Muppets.

Disney duties

Part of being a member of the Disney crew means showing up for family functions. Demi and Selena participated in the third Disney Channel Games, a five-week-long Olympics-inspired annual event that pits teams of Disney stars against each other in athletic — and often silly — competitions to raise money for charity. Selena played for The Comets team with pal Kevin Jonas as captain, and Demi played for The Lightning team, with *Camp Rock* costars Roshon Fegan and Alyson Stoner. Neither of their teams won, but during Week 3, Selena won a Fan Favorite Award. Demi performed three songs at the tie-in concert: "That's How You Know," "Get Back," and "This Is Me" with the Jonas Brothers.

Also in 2008, Selena recorded "Fly to Your Heart" for the direct-to-DVD movie *Tinker Bell*, as well as a catchy pop version of the classic song "Cruella De Vil" for the *101 Dalmatians*

Demi's phenomenal performance of the national anthem at the Dallas Cowboys Thanksgiving 2008 game brought her immense singing talent to a new audience.

Two-Disc Plantium Edition DVD. The video featured a slinky Selena strutting down a catwalk in a black and red outfit with the words "House of De Vil" splashed across the backdrop. De Vil herself made a brief cameo (shot from behind, natch).

Demi took a little time out from her own album to record "That's How You Know" on

Demi and the JoBros pose at the premiere of the brothers' film, *Jonas Brothers: The 3D Concert Experience*. Demi and the Jonas Brothers played at the Kids' Inaugural concert, which celebrated the inauguration of Barack Obama as president.

the albums *DisneyMania 6* and *Princess DisneyMania*, and covered "Wonderful Christmas Time" by Paul McCartney on Disney's holiday album *All Wrapped Up*.

In October, Selena hosted the second show of Disney Muppets *Studio DC: Almost Live*, a 30-minute music and sketch comedy special with a star-studded guest list that included Demi, and *Wizards* costars David Henrie and Jake T. Austin. A few weeks later, Demi sang the national anthem at the

Dallas Cowboys Thanksgiving Day game on November 27, 2008, when the Dallas Cowboys took on the Seattle Seahawks. The crowd roared as she sang the final notes. The Jonas Brothers performed, as well, at the halftime show.

Presidential performance

Demi joined Miley Cyrus and the Jonas Brothers at the Kids' Inaugural: We Are the Future concert at the Verizon Center in

Q: Who is Demi's manager?
A: She has three! Her stepfather, Eddie, quit his job as the manager of a Ford dealership to help manage Demi's career and travel with her. He shares duties with Kevin Jonas Sr. and Phil McIntyre, who used to coordinate concert tours for Britney Spears and currently manages the Jonas Brothers. Demi's agent is Mitchell Gossett, who also represents Miley Cyrus.

Washington, DC, on January 19, 2009, which celebrated the inauguration of President Barack Obama. First Lady Michelle Obama and Jill Biden, the Vice-President's wife, hosted the event, which was broadcast live on the Disney Channel. Tickets were scarce — most of the selected attendees were military families.

Demi was thrilled to be performing for the families of overseas troops. "It was just an honor that I could make them smile when their parents are off fighting in another country," she said. Demi wasn't sure the president elect would be able to attend, and before the show, she expressed how excited she'd be if he were actually there. "That will be the coolest thing, if Obama was watching. I think his family will be there. It would be even cooler if they were all there. But definitely, it's an honor that they even know who I am."

Michelle Obama and her daughters were there, and it was an amazing experience for Demi. "Looking down in the first row and seeing the Obamas there, it was awesome. And to see them dancing, singing, clapping, it was so surreal." When she got to meet the first family, she didn't get the chance to be starstruck because of how comfortable they made her feel. "Honestly, it was a blur, because it was like, I'm standing in the presence of the first lady, but then you kind of forgot about it because she's so normal," Demi told *MTV News*. "And she's like way down to earth. She gave me a hug, and her daughters were so sweet, and you could tell they are not fazed by anything."

Demi had wise words for the incoming president's daughters, Sasha and Malia Obama, who were coaxed by the Jonas Brothers on stage for a song. "I would give them the advice to always know that your family is there for you. You can go to your family with anything," she said. "And also, don't forget who you are. I think that's a mistake that a lot of people make. And it's something that my family keeps me from making." As a bonus tip: "Don't stop going places just because people might see you. And don't stop having sleepovers with your friends, and don't stop trick-or-treating."

fast forward

"I would love to win a Grammy one day . . . I'd also like to sky dive and maybe have my own cereal!" – Demi

Selena teamed up with her *Wizards of Waverly Place* costars — David Henrie, Jake T. Austin, and Jennifer Stone — to host the 2008–09 New Year's countdown on the Disney Channel. Stars offered their favorite moments of 2008, made predictions for 2009, and handed out awards for audience favorites on the Disney Channel, voted for through an online poll. Categories included Totally Best Guest, Totally Silly Siblings, Totally Hair-Raising and Totally Random Relatives. Guest stars included the Jonas Brothers, Miley Cyrus, and the Cheetah Girls. Demi arrived to help preview *The Princess Protection Program* and introduce the cast of *Sonny With a Chance*.

Meanwhile, Demi helped count down the final seconds of 2008 when she appeared with the Jonas Brothers and Taylor Swift on *Dick Clark's Rockin' New Year's Eve* bash in New York City's Times Square. All wearing long coats, the young stars shivered in the cold, but chatted with host Ryan Seacrest while having a great time ringing in 2009.

Entertainment Weekly listed Demi as one of 2008's breakout stars, and *Forbes Magazine* named both girls to their own

Taylor Swift, Lionel Ritchie, Ryan Seacrest, Demi, Nick, Kevin, and Joe count down the final seconds of 2008 as the ball drops in Times Square on New Year's Eve.

For the first time since *Barney*, Selena and Demi appear together in a television feature in Disney's *Princess Protection Program*.

annual list. 2009 may prove to be an even bigger year, as the costars-turned-friends are costars once again in the Disney Channel original movie *The Princess Protection Program*.

Demi plays Princess Rosalinda, a precious royal teen who is used to being the biggest fish in a very small fishbowl. When a dictator invades her tiny country, Rosalinda is whisked away to rural Wisconsin, where she must live under an assumed identity provided by the "Princess Protection Program." There she meets Carter, played by Selena, daughter of the agent who must watch over Rosalinda, who has no time for Rosalinda's regal ways. But the girls quickly find they need each other — Rosalinda in her quest to become an ordinary American teen, and tomboy Carter as she pursues a crush on the school heartthrob, uncovering her inner girlie-girl along the way.

The girls delighted in the opportunity to clash, in a comical way, on screen. "We're really excited to do our fighting scene, where me and Demi have to have this big ol' fight," Selena said on the set. "We haven't done that yet, but we've been practicing. It's just been really kind of new and different for us because we don't like fighting."

Filmed in Puerto Rico, the film costars Samantha Droke, Selena's former castmate on *Horton Hears a Who*, and Nick Braun, who recently scored a hit with the Disney original movie *Minutemen*.

Sonny With a Chance

As soon as the ball dropped on 2008, Demi hit the ground running with her brand new comedy series on the Disney Channel. "Demi Lovato — actress, singer and songwriter — is, without a doubt, the next big talent to emerge from Disney Channel," declared Disney Channel's Worldwide Entertainment president Gary Marsh when the network announced the series. Fans could hardly contain their excitement, gobbling up promotional pictures and tidbits leaked from the set.

Sonny With a Chance follows young comedian (and all-around goofball) Sonny Munroe from Green Bay, Wisconsin, to California, where she gets her big break on a sketch comedy show called *So Random*, which has a format similar to *Saturday Night Live*. "She kinda sticks out like a sore thumb, 'cause she's very quirky and very over the top," Demi says. "It's like *30 Rock*, but for the Disney Channel."

Originally titled "Welcome to Mollywood," the show sees Sonny leap to success after a

Demi and her *Sonny With a Chance* co-stars. From left to right: Brandon Smith stars as Nico, the ultimate ladies' man; Tiffany Thornton is Sonny's nemesis, Tawni Hart; pint-sized Allisyn Ashley Arm plays the zany Zora; and barrel of laughs Doug Brochu from Nickelodeon's *iCarly* stars as Duke.

funny, self-produced short film makes the rounds on the internet. She packs up and moves to Tinseltown with her mother, played by Nancy McKeon, who was a teen star herself on the sitcom *Facts of Life*. Bubbly Sonny is keen to make friends with her castmates, but one, Tawni Hart (Tiffany Thornton), seems determined to shut her out. Romantic interest is provided by the dreamy Chad Dylan Cooper (Sterling Knight), star of a popular tween drama called *MacKenzie Falls*, which films on the soundstage next to *So Random*. Between Chad's ego and the rivalry between the two shows' casts, there is plenty of fodder for comedic conflict.

Sterling Knight, who plays Chad, costarred with *High School Musical*'s Zac Efron in the movie, *17 Again*. The Houston boy, who has a background in theater, has also been seen on *The Closer*, *Grey's Anatomy*, and *Hannah Montana*.

Although her Mitchie experience at *Camp Rock* more closely mirrors Demi's own experiences, *Sonny* runs a close second. Demi says, "I think [*Sonny*] is pretty relatable because it's also a story that's similar to my life: being in a talent search and then all of a sudden getting to live your dream."

"She reminded us all of a young Mary Tyler Moore," says Adam Bonnett, Disney Channel's senior vice-president of original programming, referring to one of television's most popular actresses of all time. "She was fearless with the comedy."

"I was nervous in the beginning," Demi admits. "It's hard to carry a comedy show. If you're not funny, the show is not going to be funny. I've never had a lot of confidence in comedy, but I've really let loose and totally had fun with it. Last night, I started off really nervous and in the first take I messed up all the words. Overall, though, it turned out very well."

Becoming good friends with her new costars certainly helped. "One time, we had a food fight scene in the cafeteria at the commissary and they had these bread rolls and bagels and we were waiting to go into the scene," Demi says. "We had rolls and we were like, 'I wonder if they will ever notice if we roll a bread roll across the set?' They did."

When asked about where she expects to be in five years, Demi predicts, "Hopefully I'll still be touring and doing my TV show; obviously I'll continue that. I want to start doing movies, like feature films. And I would love to maybe direct one day."

Selena feels the music

Selena has been keeping busy recording her first studio album with Hollywood Records, and hopes to tour nationally later in 2009. "I want to do music that's fun," she told *BOP Magazine* before she entered the studio. "I don't want to do anything where people are like, 'Oh wow, she's trying to get too deep and serious.' I want something that everyone will jam out to."

Although she tends to think of herself as an actor first, singer second, "I think you can be more of yourself when you're singing," Selena says. "You can have a little bit more control over it. It's a different process, with going into the studio and not having to worry about what you look like on camera. You write music and perform it, have fun, then go on concert [tours] and jam out in front of an audience."

Like Demi, Selena finds composing her own music can be great therapy for tough times. "I believe that music is a great gateway for me to share my feelings," she says.

Selena loves
the show
Gossip Girl.

"And I enjoy writing and I enjoy playing piano a lot, so I am excited to get that next chapter of my life started. I know that it's going to be soon and I'll be able to explore that. I think my heart is in acting, but music is just an opportunity that I have been given and that I've always wanted since I was younger."

Selena stirred up chatter when she suggested one subject matter might not make it into her work. "I get so mad about ex-boyfriends, but if a boy hurts me, I don't write a song about it. They don't deserve it!" she told *OK Magazine*. She later clarified her comments on her MySpace blog. Selena wrote: "Most of my songs are about love, I am a 16-year-old teenager and I sing about what is on every girl's mind. Love. What I was implying was that the songs I sing about, the boys who have hurt me or that are no longer in my life don't deserve a song to be written about them but, that's impossible. Writing and singing is a gateway to sharing and getting out feelings."

Whatever the future holds for Selena's singing career, she remains committed to acting as her main artistic pursuit. "Acting is definitely my passion all the way," she says, although her roles may evolve as she moves into adulthood. While Selena is quick to point out that she will "always be with my Disney Channel family," she has admitted that "I would love to step out of Disney and maybe do a couple of roles — maybe challenging roles and fun roles, new things like that."

When the chance was offered to join Zac Efron and Vanessa Hudgens in their third spin around the *High School Musical*, Selena turned it down. "*High School Musical 3* is cute, and I think it would be a great opportunity for someone else," she says. "But I passed on it because I didn't want to do it. I plan to take other roles in acting that are challenging for me. After Disney, I want to be taken seriously as an actress for many years."

Selena *will* be starring in a Disney Channel original movie, however, when the film version of *Wizards of Waverly Place* hits screens soon. Titled *Wizards of Waverly Place: Stone of Dreams*, filming began in Puerto Rico in February 2009. "The plan is to have the movie ready for the 2009 calendar year," said a Disney rep in October 2008.

In 2008, Selena formed her own production company, July Moon Productions. It will allow her to buy screenplays and film rights to books, to develop for the screen for herself to star in or someone else. July Moon has already partnered with XYZ Films to produce at least two films that Selena will star in.

"Workwise, my role model is Rachel McAdams," Selena says. "I fell in love with her in the movie *Mean Girls*, I love how she spreads herself out. She did a teen movie, a romance, a comedy, a family movie, a thriller. She reinvents herself each time, and that's what I respect and love about her the most."

texas girls forever

"I'll meet other actors who are like, 'Let's go to a party.' But Selena and I would rather rent a horror movie and just eat pickles. That's our ideal sleepover. . . . It's just crazy to realize that Selena and I have known each other almost our entire lives." – Demi

Demi has said that one of her favorite memories of home is "driving around in the hot Texas sun, singing while driving with the windows down." No question Demi and Selena are strongly attached to the place where they spent their early years. "I miss Texas a lot," Selena confessed to Ellen DeGeneres, who spent her teen years in Texas. Asked by the talk show host what

things she misses, Selena said: "I miss pickles at the movie theaters!"

DeGeneres also fondly remembers eating the sour treats at theaters in her former home state, and laughed when Selena recounted a story about asking for a pickle at a California theater. The employee looked at her like she was crazy.

"When I go back home, we do the same

Demi with her little sister, Madison De La Garza, who appears on *Desperate Housewives* playing Eva Longoria's character's daughter, Juanita.

Demi's sister Madison has a puppy named Bella. Demi called it "basically 2 lbs. of adorable."

things that we always do," Selena says. "There is this park right in front of my grandma's house and believe it or not I have eighty cousins! So we all get together as a family and my grandma makes her rice, my other abuelita makes her soup, and my aunt makes her tamales. That is our moment to be together."

But as Selena and Demi's careers grow and their schedules become even more jam-packed, the opportunities to go back to Texas are fewer. Both girls have come to rely on their families to create a sense of home wherever they are. "My sister Madison and I are always together," Demi says. "I am always quoting her. [And my sister] Dallas — both are very caring and honest. I know that I can always ask them anything and they will give me their best opinion."

Asked how she copes with her workload and the tremendous pressure of living a very public life, Demi says: "It's definitely my parents, and it's definitely the way that I was raised. I've got a great family. My support system includes my best friends, which now includes my cast, and I went to church every Sunday. My faith is strong, and my parents are incredible. They're there for me. I can talk to them about anything, no matter what. If I were to say, 'I quit today,' if I were to walk out of this room and say, 'I don't want to act. I don't want to do anything anymore,' my mom would say, 'All right. Let's go back to school.' They're one hundred percent supportive, but yet they don't push me to do anything. I love them to death. They're amazing."

Of course, it helps to have a best friend to see you through it all. In Hollywood friendships can be as fleeting as fashion trends, but Demi and Selena's has been solid since the first time they laid eyes on each other at that long-ago talent search in Texas. Since then, their careers have careened along parallel courses, with no signs of slowing down or heading off in different directions. The girls are often photographed with their arms around each other or gripping hands as though they are afraid to let go. Perhaps they never will. As Demi says of Selena, "She is my rock."

SELENA'S FILMOGRAPHY AND DISCOGRAPHY

Films

Year	Film	Role
2003	*Spy Kids 3D: Game Over*	Waterpark Girl
2005	*Walker, Texas Ranger: Trial By Fire*	Julie
2008	*Horton Hears a Who!*	Mayor's Daughter
2008	*Another Cinderella Story**	Mary Santiago
2009	*The Princess Protection Program**	Carter

*Disney Channel original movie

Television

Year	Show	Role
2001–2002	*Barney & Friends*	Gianna
2007	*What's Stevie Thinking?*	Stevie
2007	*Arwin!*	Alexa
2007–present	*Wizards of Waverly Place*	Alex Russo

Guest appearances

Year	Show	Role
2006	*The Suite Life of Zack & Cody* (Season 2, Episode 21)	Gwen
2007	*Hannah Montana* (Season 2, Episode 13)	Mikayla
2007	*Hannah Montana* (Season 2, Episode 18)	Mikayla
2008	*Jonas Brothers: Living the Dream* (Season 1, Episode 7)	Herself
2008	*Disney Channel Games 2008*	Herself
2008	*Studio DC: Almost Live*	Herself

Discography

Year	Album
2006	*Brain Zapped* (soundtrack)
2008	*Another Cinderella Story* (soundtrack)

Year	Single
2007	"Everything Is Not What It Seems," *Wizards of Waverly Place*
2008	"Cruella De Vil," *DisneyMania 6*
2008	"Fly to Your Heart," *Tinker Bell*

DEMI'S FILMOGRAPHY AND DISCOGRAPHY

Films

Year	Film	Role
2008	*Camp Rock**	Mitchie Torres
2009	*Jonas Brothers: The 3D Concert Experience*	Herself
2009	*The Princess Protection Program**	Rosalinda / Rosie
2009	*Camp Rock 2**	Mitchie Torres

*Disney Channel Original Movie

Television

Year	Show	Role
2001–2002	*Barney & Friends*	Angela
2007	*As the Bell Rings*	Charlotte Adams
2009	*Sonny With a Chance*	Sonny Munroe

Guest appearances

Year	Show	Role
2006	*Prison Break* (Season 2, Episode 4)	Danielle Curtin
2007	*Just Jordan* (Season 2, Episode 6)	Nicole
2008	*Jonas Brothers: Living the Dream* (Season 1, Episode 3)	Herself
2008	*Jonas Brothers: Living the Dream* (Season 1, Episode 7)	Herself
2008	*Disney Channel Games 2008*	Herself
2008	*Studio DC: Almost Live*	Herself

Discography

Year	Album
2008	*Don't Forget*
2008	*Camp Rock* (soundtrack)

Year	Single
2008	"That's How You Know," *DisneyMania 6* and *Princess Disney Mania*

Living the Dream
Hannah Montana and Miley Cyrus — The Unofficial Story

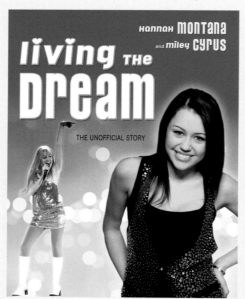

Get the scoop on the girl behind that world-famous smile in *Living the Dream*, the first backstage look at Miley Cyrus and *Hannah Montana*. Miley's story is all captured here: her life before *Hannah*, her albums (and Hannah's too), the Best of Both Worlds tour, the *Hannah Montana* movie, and a month-by-month look at Miley's meteoric rise to superstardom. Featuring tons of full-color photos of Miley and her friends and family (some never published before!), plus bios of Billy Ray Cyrus (Robby Ray), Jason Earles (Jackson), Emily Osment (Lilly), Mitchel Musso (Oliver) and more, *Living the Dream* also includes a *Hannah Montana* episode guide full of fun facts and bloopers! Sweet niblets!

All in This Together
The Unofficial Story of *High School Musical*

You've memorized the lyrics and know all the dance moves. Time to find out the story behind the scenes of *High School Musical*! *All in This Together* offers the first look at how the movie got made, bios of the six stars — Zac Efron (Troy), Vanessa Hudgens (Gabriella), Ashley Tisdale (Sharpay), Corbin Bleu (Chad), Monique Coleman (Taylor) and Lucas Grabeel (Ryan) — an exciting look at their solo careers plus dozens of full color never-before-seen photos of the cast. If you're a fan of *High School Musical*, this is the book you've been looking for!

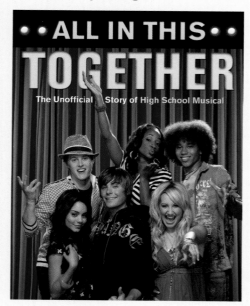

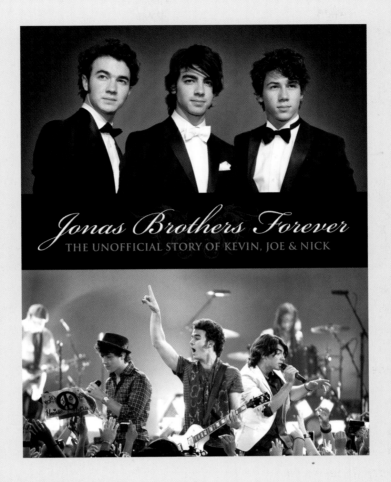

Jonas Brothers Forever

The Unofficial Story of Kevin, Joe & Nick

There's simply no stopping Kevin, Joe and Nick Jonas. Jam-packed with color photos, *Jonas Brothers Forever: The Unofficial Story of Kevin, Joe & Nick* is the only complete guide to the amazing world of the JoBros: the life and career of this talented trio; their family, friends and the importance of their faith; their albums, videos, tours and TV shows. With a special feature on *Camp Rock* and Demi Lovato, *Jonas Brothers Forever* is tailor-made for fans who happily suffer from Obsessive Jonas Disorder.

Visit ecwpress.com for an announcement about our upcoming book on *iCarly*'s Miranda Cosgrove!